NEW WINE, OLD WINESKINS

New Wine, Old Wineskins

The Catholic Church and Change in Ireland Today

MARTIN TIERNEY

VERITAS

First published 2008 by
Veritas Publications
7/8 Lower Abbey Street
Dublin 1
Ireland
Email publications@veritas.ie
Website www.veritas.ie

ISBN 978 1 84730 059 1

10 9 8 7 6 5 4 3 2 1

A catalogue record for this book is available from the British Library.

Cover: *The Marriage at Cana*, from a series of Scenes of the New Testament (fresco) by Barna da Siena (fl.1350–55).
(Collegiata, San Gimignano, Italy/Alinari/The Bridgeman Art Library)

Printed in the Republic of Ireland by Betaprint, Dublin

Veritas books are printed on paper made from the wood pulp of managed forests. For every tree felled, at least one tree is planted, thereby renewing natural resources.

Contents

Foreword

It has become clichéd to talk any more about the rapidity of change. There is hardly an aspect of change that hasn't touched our daily lives. All of us are caught up in this vortex. Making sense of what is happening is what very few of us has enough time or the capacity to achieve. We are part of something we yet don't fully understand. We can be frightened, hopeful and anxious, all within the space of a day! The Catholic Church too has experienced the harsh wind of change, at times with unfortunate consequences. I welcome the publication of *New Wine, Old Wineskins*. For many years Martin Tierney has been writing and reflecting on a changing Church in a changing society, both in the secular and the religious press. He tries to 'push the boat out' a little in his analysis of the cultural forces that are operating in a new global society of which our church is so much a part. Occasionally his individualistic style and approach to life make his intrepretation of current events controversial. He may annoy but he seldom bores! These articles from his regular and widely read column in the *Irish Catholic* newspaper certainly provide food for thought and reflection. There is a freshness in his approach that makes these most readable articles thought provoking. I wish, *New Wine, Old Wineskins: The Catholic Church and Change in Ireland Today*, every success. It offers an analysis not just of the church's immediate troubles and successes, but of other forces operating below the surface of a once-powerful institution that ruled the lives of many people. It is said that the media is the 'first rough draft of history'. It provides an on-the-spot interpretation of currents events. This book will contribute in some small measure to our relfections on the extraordinary world in which we seek to proclaim the 'good news' of God's love for all people.

Bishop James Moriarty
Bishop of Kildare and Leighlin.

A Child of Vatican Two

The name of Pope John XXIII will forever be associated
with a Momentous Council that gave hope to the Church.

Only once can I recall crying at the death of a complete stranger. He was a fat, genial eighty-two-year-old man! When he died in 1963, I knelt and prayed and wept. It was like a death in the family. He was the son of a poor farmer, whose birthplace was shared with six cows. In spirit he is still a father to me. As with the death of J.F. Kennedy, I can recall with clarity where I was when I first heard that this universally loved man had passed on to God. His name was Pope John XXIII. He came, like John the Baptist, to bear witness to the light; to make the rough ways plain, to prepare a path, to show Christ to the world; like his master, his mission was short, cut off by death. Shortly before his death he said, 'every day is a good day to be born, every day is a good day to die. I know in whom I have believed'. He went to meet his end with the serenity of a child going home, knowing that his father was waiting there with open arms.

I am a child of the Second Vatican Council, ordained over forty years. I look back with sadness, even with a tinge of disillusionment, for what might have been, but with thankfulness for what was. For 'what was' I give thanks above all to God and to Pope John XXIII. More than any other pope he wanted dialogue with the world, irrespective of creed. He once introduced himself to Jewish visitors to the Vatican with the greeting, 'I am Joseph your brother'. It was this pope who struggled to unravel the growing centralisation of the Church. To one cardinal he is reported to have said *sono nel sacco qui* ('I'm in a bag here'). Unfortunately, this strategy of decentralisation has been strenuously reversed under the succeeding Pontificates. Peter no longer trusts the other disciples.

John was a gentle revolutionary. Far from being the caretaker that the Church expected, John created an atmosphere in which, 'a lot of things came unstuck – old patterns of thought, behaviour and feeling'. In place of dogmatic answers, John asked questions and encouraged others to join him in finding out whether old forms were still the right forms. He raised great sprawling questions and he shared with others in finding answers. We don't ask questions any more. There is no one there to listen! In forty years I have seen the pendulum swing right back. Such is life!

There are some things that never change. The work of a priest is centred on the Eucharist – sacrifice and sacrament. Jesus, 'the bread of life', is the source and centre, both of the motivation for priesthood and the ministry he exercises for others. Questions will always swirl around the life of the Church but the hunger for God remains. Over the forty years, on a purely personal level, the struggle to communicate the Gospel, build community and be life-giving as a person has become

MARTIN TIERNEY

much more challenging in recent times. With backs-against-the-wall, the priesthood places more demands on the person, but is arguably more fulfilling today. People are people, their fundamental needs change little. The enormous cultural changes that have taken place over the last few decades appear to me to demand the attention of another Vatican Council, even more open than the last one. Wouldn't it be wonderful if a Council, representative of all the members of the Church, could be convened to address current issues in the light of the Gospel?

I was ordained into the priesthood at a time of energy, hope and buoyant optimism. '*Aggiornamento*' ('bringing up to date') was the buzz word of the day. Everything was possible. Pope John had produced documents that were extraordinary at that time. His last encyclical, *Pacem in Terris*, was uncharacteristically addressed not to the bishops of the Church, but to 'all men of good will'. It welcomed the progressive improvement of conditions for working people, the involvement of women in politics, the decline of imperialism and the growth of national self-determination. All these were signs of a growing liberation.

Within a tiny phrase like the 'People of God' (now frowned on in the Vatican) the possibility of a new model of Church emerging from the Council became more than a dream. We foolishly thought that the angles of the pyramid could be rounded. Certainly, there was over-optimism and mistakes, but little is built without risk. The priest draws his life as much, or more, from the people he serves as from the Church. They have been wonderful.

As Frank Sinatra sings, 'Regrets, I've had a few. But then again, too few to mention'. I do think celibacy should be optional –

I believe this would make for a more rounded priesthood. Collegiality: I regret that it has never been tried and I am doubtful if I will live to see its implementation. These regrets are outweighed by the goodness of God and the wonderful people I have been privileged to meet over forty years.

ADVERTISING AND SOAPS

The Gospel has to be sold. The good news is competing for attention with many other voices. The world of advertising and 'soaps' may have something to teach church people through the strategies they use to meet their potential market.

We all live inside our own little worlds. We may even deceive ourselves that it is the only world where anything is happening. It is so easy to become locked in an ecclesiastical closet and fail to observe that the big wide world is changing faster than we can imagine. There are times when I feel consoled that what our Church is experiencing is not unique. A recent newspaper column, written by a politician, could just as easily be applied to the Church and indeed to many voluntary organisations:

It all happened very suddenly. Twenty years ago most political parties had no difficulty getting people to do the ordinary things of everyday politics – deliver election literature, canvass, man polling stations, put up (and where possible pull down) election posters and of course sell the inevitable tickets for draws and functions. In addition people attended monthly meetings of their branch or cumann and for the most part had a sturdy loyalty to the party of their allegiance. Today's branch and cumann meetings are a pale shadow of their former selves. Many branches exist only on paper, meeting on a sporadic basis, if at all … It is as if people looked for a quick fix and, not finding it, simply melted away.

Sounds familiar, does it not?

Our world is changing fast. Here are a few examples. Life expectancy has risen by over ten years for males since 1940. When I was going to UCD in the 1950s the number of full-time students at universities in the country was only 7,900. The number of students at third-level colleges and universities today is 112,200! The number of births outside marriage has risen from 4 per cent in 1978 to over 28 per cent today. There are now over 32,000 cohabiting couples in Ireland.

I was born in 1938. This was closer to the First World War, which was history to me, than a person born in 1964 is to the Second Vatican Council. For many people under forty, the Council is history. Yet when I go to meetings I hear the Second Vatican Council mentioned as if it was yesterday. To the majority of people in Ireland today it exists only in a historical twilight! Who can recall the wall map in school with the pink of the Empire ringing the world? The sun has now set on the Empire. It's history. The burning question is how can we as a

Church change and adapt to a culture that, let's face it, is foreign to most of us. More than half of the priests in the Dublin Diocese are over fifty-six years of age. The temptation is to retire mentally because we can no loner cope with an ever-changing landscape.

This new landscape of life was brilliantly portrayed in RTÉ's 'soap' *Bachelor's Walk*. It got inside the heads of twenty- and thirtysomethings. These are some of the young people to whom we are attempting to preach the Gospel. The language and vocabulary was almost foreign to me.

'Advertising,' said Herbert Zeltner, a New York marketing consultant, 'has a dual role: one part is to make people want a product, the other is to tell them it is available and where it can be found.' This is the business we are in! The Gospel has to be sold. People need to know that it is indeed 'the pearl of great price'. To adjust to this kind of marketspeak isn't easy. The voice of the Church is one voice competing against many, without the resources or personnel available to the advertiser. How can we get our voice heard?

In 1987 the amount spent in the US and Europe on advertising was over $4 billion! In pursuit of why and how people are prompted to buy, millions of consumers are watched, quizzed, divided and examined in almost every conceivable group and subgroup. Trends are continually charted and analysed to help determine which products are likely to become ripe for selling. For instance one such survey showed widespread underlying concern among people about social isolation and rejection. From this it was decided that there was a bright future for what is called 'social supports' – health clubs, vacations, games. Hey presto, the entrepreneur latched on to these things and are now making big bucks!

The evangelical churches know that word-of-mouth evangelism is what brings people to God. People who themselves have been touched by God become in turn the best evangelists. Encouraging people to speak out, telling of the mighty things that God has done in one's life, is the best invitation to others to seek 'the pearl of great price'. We can learn from contemporary business methods. There is no doubt that 'the children of this generation are wiser than the children of light' (Lk 16:8).

Anniversary of Dietrich Bonhoeffer

One of the most remarkable figures to emerge with honour from World War Two was Pastor Dietrich Bonhoeffer. He was executed, leaving behind memories that have inspired generations of Christians.

I have had a book on my shelf for forty-five years. It stares out at me as I write. This book has frightened me, challenged me and inspired me; it haunts me most days. I bought it in my first flush of zeal as a young seminarian. *The Cost of Discipleship*, by German Protestant theologian Dietrich Bonhoeffer, was truly an eye-opener to me! In this classic work, Bonhoeffer argues that, 'cheap grace is the mortal enemy of our Church. Our struggle today is for costly grace'. As a young seminarian I was frightened by the demands of living the gospel to the full. When one stares the demands of the gospel full in the face it is difficult not to hunt for a rationalised bolt-hole to escape the implications of what Jesus asks of us. Over the years I have learned through reading and re-reading this book that it is easier to debate religion than to live it. Bonhoeffer is frightening because he chose costly grace and paid for it with his life. With people like

Maximillian Kolbe and Romero, Bonhoeffer was prepared to pay the ultimate price for the God he loved. If Protestants canonised saints, Bonhoeffer would be one today. He was born a century ago and is one of the best-known Christians of the twentieth century. He is one of ten martyrs commemorated above the door of Westminster Abbey. His family home is now a museum and several tourist companies offer 'pilgrimages' to sites with which he is associated. He is also a person who has fed the spiritual lives of Christians of all denominations.

Dietrich Bonhoeffer was born in February 1906 in Breslau (now Wrocław in Poland). He entered a Germany in which Bismarck's land-owning class still had politics in its grip. He came from a privileged family and grew up in the educated milieu of Berlin University. By the age of twenty-four, after studying theology, he was a university lecturer. He was ordained the following year. When Hitler became Chancellor, Bonhoeffer put his faith in the Church to provide the opposition that would confront the evils of Nazism. He headed a seminary for training pastors for the illegal Confessing Church, established in opposition to the pro-Nazi state church. In 1936 the Gestapo began to move against him, withdrawing his licence to speak in public and closing the seminary, so he moved to America. He could have remained as a respectable pastor in America, but Bonhoeffer was too transparent a Christian to remain there while his people suffered under Nazism. He lived what he wrote: 'the disciple is dragged out of his relative security into a life of absolute insecurity; from a life which is observable and calculable into a life where everything is unobservable and fortuitous; out of the realm of the finite into the realm of infinite possibilities.'

He returned to Germany on the eve of war and agreed to join the anti-Nazi conspiracy. In 1943 Bonhoeffer was arrested and imprisoned. Evidence linked him with the attempt on Hitler's life. Finally he was summarily tried and in April 1945 he was hanged in Flossenburg concentration camp. Bonhoeffer wrote that the Christian, 'tormented by sin, weakness and death, stands by God in his agony'.

There is an extraordinary timelessness about the writings of Bonhoeffer. He gave a lot of thought to how Christians might conform themselves to Christ in a post-war, non-religious age. If anything his uncompromising stance is more relevant in our neo-liberal times. According to Bonhoeffer, 'cheap grace is the preaching of forgiveness without requiring repentance, baptism without church discipline, communion without confession, absolution without personal confession. Cheap grace is grace without discipleship, grace without the cross, grace without Jesus Christ, living and incarnate'. He wrote that what people were looking for was 'grace at the cheapest price'. In the recent past people claim that it was the fear of God rather than love that inspired them to goodness. God was the judge, the avenger, the punisher. Could it be that the pendulum has swung to the other extreme? The demands of love require sacrifice. Love of necessity places constrictions on human behaviour. Understanding love as a decision for Christ means embracing the cross, the very opposite of 'cheap grace'. Bonhoeffer is a man for every age.

ARCHBISHOP MILINGO
– A MAVERICK OR A SAINT?

*Archbishop Milingo has been a thorn in the side of the
Vatican for many years. Maybe he does have a message
for the Church which fails to listen.*

Archbishop Milingo has done it again! Jumped over the wall –
this time for good? He recently slipped his Vatican minders
and appeared unsuspectingly at the National Press Club in
Washington, where he immediately headed up a new organisation
entitled 'Married Priests Now'.

I have an interest in Milingo, whose story poses a threat to
the unity of the Church. In 1969 Pope Paul VI consecrated him
as bishop of the Archdioceses of Lusaka, the capital of Zambia.
He was one of Africa's youngest bishops. He served there for
fourteen years. In the 1970s on a visit to Zambia I had an
opportunity of meeting the Archbishop on two occasions, and
of attending his healing services. I found him friendly, articulate,
excitable and genuinely spiritual. His problem was that he took
the Lord's injunction to his disciples to go out 'to preach and to
heal' too seriously. Unlike the early Church few people today
believe that the healing power of Jesus is still active and effective

in the world. One early Church Father, Origen, wrote how Christians 'expel evil spirits, and perform many cures'. He also claimed that, 'the name of Jesus can still remove distractions from the minds of men, and expel demons, and also take away diseases'. To offer healing is one way in which Christians can express that love which is so much needed by people today. Milingo always knew this.

He became famous as an exorcist and a powerful spiritual healer. His house in Lusaka was large. It had an upper mezzanine floor reached by a wide staircase. On the landing off this floor were numerous rooms. On the days he held his healing service every place was jammed packed. Colourfully dressed women with children, old people, the emaciated poor of all ages and the seriously ill blocked every accessible space. There was a cacophony of noise. When did you last hear of an Episcopal residence crammed with the sick and the poor? I recall the Archbishop's copious use of holy water (buckets full!). I believe that later he began to use other symbolic agents, such as honey, for his services. This may have ultimately led to his downfall. The whole scene was like something from a Cecil B. DeMille movie.

In 1983 Milingo was recalled to Rome because of controversy over his 'non-conventional' healing ministry. I attended one of his healing services in Rome and I was astonished at the numbers who came. The individual and the world is in such need of spiritual healing that anything or anyone who offers hope will attract crowds. In Rome, Pope John Paul II protected the Archbishop's charism. He appeared on Italian TV and radio shows and conducted healing Masses throughout Europe that attracted thousands of people. This did not sit well with some bishops in Rome. The more his ministry grew, the more his freedom to celebrate Mass was restricted. 'Just because something is good, and for the welfare of the Lord, doesn't mean it won't meet opposition,' Milingo said.

Despite his great love for the Roman Catholic Church, the Archbishop's public call for an end to mandatory celibacy in 2001, punctuated by his very public marriage to a Doctor of Acupuncture from Korea, was rejected as an embarrassment. At the time he was under the influence of the Moonies. Milingo wasn't the first priest to be attracted to the Moonies. A good priest of the Dublin Diocese joined the Moonies and later attained a significant position of influence within the Unification Church. Milingo returned to Rome from America, apparently renouncing his marriage, and was received with compassion and understanding by Pope John Paul. However, the extremely strict regime he was forced to live under and the constant surveillance he had to endure finally led to his latest break with Rome.

Milingo claims that 'currently on the sideline, there are approximately 150,000 validly ordained priests. But these priests are married. The majority of these priests are ready, and willing to return to the sacred ministry of the altar. It is our mission to find a way to reconcile these married priests with the Church and to reinstate them in the public sacred ministry'. This idea is anathema to Rome.

At the time of writing, the big fear is that Milingo could consecrate priests to the episcopacy and thereby start a new schismatic church. If he did so in Zambia, such a move would have serious repercussions for the local Catholic Church.

MARTIN TIERNEY

BEING SINGLE

The Church seems to have little regard for those who remain single through choice or circumstances. A rethink is urgently needed.

There was a time in the recent past when if you weren't married or co-habiting by thirty, then you were on the shelf. You were considered a bit of a misfit. Back then it was not publicly admitted, but to be a single person was considered to have failed in life. People talked about single people with pity, in whispers, and never in their company. Terms like spinster and old maid conjured up images of fussy middle-aged women prying into everyone else's business. Even widows have told me that once you're single you are a misfit. Separated women were considered either 'fair game' or a challenge to existing relationships. Invitations could dry up. Socialising could be confined, albeit not by choice, to a diminishing circle of friends and relations.

Nowadays all this has changed. Many people are now single by choice. We know that it is possible to be a success in marriage and a success in the single life, a failure in marriage and a failure in the single life.

However, some of the pain and insecurity felt by those who are single can be attributed to the insensitivity of married people. What I call 'nappy talk' can, on occasion, be hurtful to a single person present. There are still single people who long to be married and have children. A total centering on the child in arms by doting parents can be unwittingly tedious or even hurtful.

In the day before murders were two-a-penny I have a dim memory of a baby being taken from a pram outside a shop in Camden Street in the late 1950s. The story was huge, and ran for days and days. The culprit was a young woman who longed for a child of her own.

The Church remains mute about the single life. Sermons invariably direct their message to the marrieds and to young people. I know many single people feel hurt; they have told me so. A mature single person remarked to me recently 'as far as the Church is concerned I am a nobody'.

Single people frequently live lives of extraordinary generosity. I had an aunt who died at the age of 82. Her peaceful death took place in the sparsely but adequately furnished room of an old peoples' home in rural Ireland. As soon as news of her last illness percolated through the family they all converged on her bedside. She was single and a woman of dignity, faith and love. Her 'singleness' had allowed her to share resources of love and compassion far wider than the care of a family would ever had permitted. In addition she cared for her ailing mother, my grandmother, with singular generosity. Her family was everyone else's family as well. She straddled time and eternity, because, after all, the only thing that lasts after everything has passed away is love. And she was full of it. We loved her very much.

I have also met the introspective frigidity of a single life curled up in bitterness. A single life full of unfulfilled possibilities, a prison of self-pity, springing from genuine hurts of the past, must surely be hell on earth. It is a basic rule that when the self becomes unlocked and opens out to give, it will be able to receive in exact proportion to its generosity.

Our church doesn't often recognise and acknowledge the love and generosity of single people. Many of the lay people who help around parishes are single, often widows and widowers. When did you last hear a Prayer of the Faithful for single people? We have sermons on marriage but never on the single life. Why is this? We tend to forget those who are separated or divorced, in addition to those single by choice or circumstances. This is a pity. It is not a matter of malice rather forgetfulness.

CARING FOR THE EARTH

The Church is well placed, especially at the local level,
to encourage a climate of care for the environement.

Kilkee. My tongue touching the roof of my mouth to shape the
name of the place, remembers the taste of candyfloss and
perriwinkles, bullseyes and lemonade, the Pollock Holes and the
Hydro ballroom. Scott's pub on the main street remains just as it
was fifty years ago. Kilkee calls out to the ghosts of my parents to
return once more into the sunshine and the carefree days of
youth. Recently I drove through Kilkee on my way to say Mass
in that evocative Church at Kilbaha with its historic Ark. Such
places were long ago wiped clean with the baleful tears of
generations, whose descendents are now scattered to the four
winds. Where over 12,000 peasants huddled fearfully from
hunger and the landlord, scarcely a thousand of their descendents
remain. At Kilbaha, the ruins of Marcus Keane's house still
stands gaunt like a dying tree in a barren landscape. Keane, the
land agent, was responsible for so many having to take the coffin
ships to God-knows-where. For a month every year we filled our
city lungs with air that smelled of seaweed, turf and dung from

the fields. It was on the golf course at George's Head, perched high on the cliffs, threateningly exposed to the Atlantic gales, that I first learned the hard lesson of losing gracefully. We stayed in 'lodges' that soon became as sandy as a butcher's floor. Housekeeping was not a priority. Kilkee is still a wonderful place. It was here we kept our souls. The same was true of Richard Harris, the actor, whose statue struts an athletic pose at the Diamond Rocks.

In Celtic Tiger Ireland there is a dark side emerging. In 1990 the number of houses in Kilkee was 596, out of which 428 were occupied all the year round In eight years from 1992 to 2000, 795 new houses were built. Kilkee now has an occupancy rate of 34.2 per cent. A new ghost town encircles the existing village with loveless embrace. The same is true right across the western sea board. It still goes on. In the past we had deserted famine villages, now we have the gloomy emptiness of glamorous homes lived in for a few short weeks each year. The occasional occupants are not stakeholders in the local community. At weekends, many seaside towns and villages are transformed into the rombustiousness of a Dawson City's lawlessness and alcohol steeped 'craic'! Fr Sean McDonagh, a doughty ecological campaigner, has painstakingly detailed what has happened in Co. Clare in a talk, 'Are we Deaf to the Cry of the Earth?', which he gave at the Céifin Conference in 2000.

There is now a hue and cry about 'global warming'. But are we concerned because our own way of life is threatened or because we see the earth as God's gift to be treasured lovingly? Our fearfulness may be because the 'God' of 'economic growth' may be halted and the rich will no longer be able to get richer. As

Christians I wonder do we need to repent of our contribution to destroying the earth? We are stewards of creation. Future generations are unlikely to thank us for our part in destroying their legacy. The church has an opportunity to give leadership in the present ecological crisis. Each parish can promote an ethic of care for the local environment and encourage non-church people to participate. It appears to me that there are parishes that take this seriously. Even in the care and beauty of many church grounds it is obvious that there is an increased consciousness of the gift of God to us in the beauty of nature. The world was created by a personal God who declares that it is good and loves his creation. Jesus lived lightly on the earth.

Psalm 19 wonderfully expresses the inner cry in the face of the beauty of nature:

> The heavens declare the glory of God,
> And the firmament proclaims his handiwork
> Day pours out the word today
> And night to night imparts knowledge.

Woodie Guthrie sang:

> I've roamed and rambled and I've followed my footsteps
> To the sparkling sands of her diamond deserts
> And all around me a voice was sounding
> This land was made for you and me.

THE CHANGING FACE OF THE PRIESTHOOD IN IRELAND

Fifty years ago seminaries were turning away candidates for the priesthood. Now it is usual to look forward to fill the gaps left by a declining number of priests.

As I grow older it becomes more difficult to put shape or sense into the changes of the last fifty years. Take ordinations for instance. Recently three men, all over forty, were ordained for the Dublin Diocese. That's good news. In the late 1950s and early 1960s, however, Dublin's diocesan seminary of Holy Cross College was like a battery chicken farm. It was so full that each year in June, a cull of seminarians 'inappropriate for the Dublin Diocese' took place to keep the student numbers down. In 1960 there were one hundred and nine students in the College studying for the priesthood. If one is to include those studying in Maynooth and Rome, the complete complement of seminarians for Dublin was about one hundred and fifty at any one time! In one year alone, 1960, a staggering forty students entered the College as aspiring priests for the Dublin Diocese. So plentiful were the priests in the 1950s that most had to go abroad for some time before a position became available for them in the diocese. It was always made clear to us, 'If you want to leave, there are any number of people waiting to take your place'. So what happened? Did God say 'Enough is enough' and stop calling young men to follow him? If God is still calling, are huge numbers of young men not listening or refusing to answer the call? Of course, it could be that, in the past, many entered the seminary for all the wrong reasons. Many of them, in their declining years, may now be living lives of quiet desperation. Having been toppled from the pedestals of exaggerated deference and obsequiousness, and joined the human race, the priesthood may now look a lot less attractive to potential candidates. Having a 'priest in the family' is hardly a badge of honour any more!

According to SJ Connolly in *Priests and People in Pre-Famine Ireland*, there were 1,640 diocesan clergy in Ireland for a population of between four and five million. This grew significantly and in 1849 there were 2,400 diocesan priests in Ireland. Today, there are 3,168 diocesan clergy for a slightly larger population. So we are better off by far than we were two hundred years ago – before the car, the internet, the telephone. The demands made on priests do not seem to have been as onerous back then. One commentator wrote in 1834, 'Having abandoned the simpler style of living of former times, the country priest now copes with the country Squire, keeps sporting dogs, controls elections, presides at political clubs and sits 'cheek by jowl' at public dinners and public assemblies with Peers of the Realm' (*Peel, Priests and Politics* by Donal Kerr). In *Mo Scéal Féin*, written in the nineteenth century by Fr Peter O'Leary, it appears that horseback rides over long distances to attend to the sick took up a lot of the priest's time. Now every sacrament has an attending preparation programme, liturgies demand careful attention, deaths and especially funerals can no longer be the perfunctory events they were long ago. The people rightly expect more of their priests. The main change over the years is the growing habit of celebrating Mass for all and every occasion. In the nineteenth century a parish was grateful if one Mass was celebrated each Sunday for the faithful of the area. Now we enter huge cavernous churches, with a scattering of people, having Mass celebrated for them at their most convenient time.

With the age profile of the priests steadily creeping upwards there will be a need for lay people to take on a more pivotal role in the Church. After the Second Vatican Council the Irish bishops issued a statement claiming that the laity would have to be more involved 'in the spiritual ministry of the Church'. This hasn't really happened. I would like to know what the bishops meant by 'spiritual ministry'? Is it praying for the sick, proclaiming the Word of God, consoling the bereaved, preaching and teaching, or is it moving the chairs in the parish hall before the next meeting? For nearly a quarter of a century there has been talk of collaborative ministry in the Church, yet many parishes are still ruled and governed in all aspects by the parish priest. In the very near future this will no longer be viable. Real progress is frustrated by the fact that on every level in the Church, laity only have an advisory role. To give lay people a decision-making possibility at different levels would make them stakeholders in an organisation in which they are now simply participators or spectators.

Choosing a Denomination

It is becoming the norm for parents not to have their children baptised but to leave the decision to the child in adulthood.

There was real anguish in her voice. The sighs indicated pain, even frustration. I wasn't sure. 'When do you do baptisms?' she asked. 'Sunday,' I replied, conscious that the clock was ticking towards ten when I had to be on the altar. 'Sunday,' she repeated after me. A long pause followed. 'I'm a grandmother,' she said. 'My daughter has just had a new baby. She doesn't want it baptised. She says if the child wants religion she can decide for herself when she is old enough,' she blurted out. I understood better where the grandmother was coming from when she said, 'I had the others baptised but she wasn't interested.' Following a long pause she said, 'We'll see,' and sighed abruptly before putting down the phone.

This is not a unique story: it is being repeated throughout the country. At chic dinner parties, and in local hostelries, people sometimes nod knowingly to one another and say, 'I'd let them decide for themselves about God. I wouldn't force it down their throats'. They are passing on to their children the only religion they know: the religion of choice. They will raise their children to have choices; to survey the goods and make the best choice. Religion is but one choice in a world of choices.

Religion for me is my beginning. It is the soil in which I was planted. It is what happens every day. It is the prayers I say or don't say. It is the questions I ask, the rituals I perform. It is my parents. It is Sunday and Holy Days of Obligation. It is seasons. It is frustrations with what happens or doesn't happen in Rome. It is bad singing. It is my siblings. It is my identity. It is my limitations. It is my fears as well as my hopes. But I choose God. I choose God and fight and question him. I choose God and ask him – is it true? I was born and raised a Roman Catholic. I believe this wasn't an accident. Just as I am and always will be a Tierney, I am, and always will be, a Catholic.

Being a Catholic still leaves me with huge questions. It gives me the courage to ask these. Being a Catholic is in the fibre of my being, just as being Irish is, and even if I were to leave the Church, I know it would never leave me. There are other things that won't leave me either; some of these are simple things – how to hold a knife and fork; having respect for my elders; not talking with my mouth full; sharing when I have more than enough for myself; always saying please and thank you; being honest and truthful; turning out the lights when they are not needed; visiting the sick – come to think of it, I learned these as a child at home and I cannot recall being given a choice!

In every home there is a whole range of options about which no choice is given. Some of them I listed above. Then there are the areas of choice, usually extremely limited, within which falls religion. Why is 'religion' becoming more and more a matter of choice with young people? Choosing a Church suitable to your disposition is the latest popular fad. A 'Catholic' man boasted to me recently how all his adolescent children now attended an Evangelical Church in the city centre. 'More life there,' he claimed. Even some priests have changed denomination as a matter of choice. Of course, this may have had more to do with celibacy than doctrine or disposition. Nevertheless, we will see increased traffic between denominations as people 'shop around' for the Church that best suits them. The best preacher, the best music, the shortest homily, the best community, are rapidly becoming the criteria on which choice of Church is based. This is happening already in the cities and in time will percolate to the rural areas.

The buzzword in business in terms of marketing a product successfully is the USP (unique selling point): what has this product got that others haven't? Supermarkets constantly encourage 'impulse buying' by the strategic placement of goods within easy reach, usually 'line of sight'. In the make-believe world of the supermarkets a glittering Disneyland entices the buyer to select and buy (watch for the strategic lighting at the deli counter!) They discourage thought or reflection and appeal only to the senses.

I suppose it is hard for some people who are so beguiled by the world of commerce not to take their religion as another product; another matter of choice; a 'take it or leave it decision'. The search for truth, the deep reflection needed where God is concerned is truly difficult in the fickle, fleeting world of today.

MARTIN TIERNEY

Clergy are Too Shy to Evangelise

A recent survey among clergy of the reformed churches revealed a shyness to proclaim the Gospel with boldness.

A recent survey of Anglican, Baptist and Methodist clergy in England showed that most clergymen are introverts who lack the characteristics to be 'out there' in the community. In fact they are too shy to go out and convert people to Christianity. When the clergymen began their ministry most considered evangelisation to be an important part of what they were expected to do. However, over the years, clergy of all denominations became bogged down in running services, dealing with the organist and keeping the church rainproof. They despaired at the onward march of secularism and their own inability to come to grips with the prevailing culture and so they simply gave up on any attempts to entice the unaffiliated to become Christian. The study, conducted by Bishop Michael Whinny, retired Bishop of Southwell, showed that personality type may also play a part in the reluctance of many clergy to go out knocking on doors and winning new converts. He found that the introverted clergy were more at home in traditional, contemplative and structured worship styles, while extroverted and more spontaneous ministers were happier in the freer, participative style of the fast-growing younger churches. The research indicated that, while in the general population 47 per cent of people are introverted, among Anglican clergy the proportion rose to 62 per cent. All three denominations surveyed are experiencing long-term decline, although within each there are pockets of revival, normally led by evangelical clergy who would be classified under the extrovert personality type. He added that, in spite of low morale, few ministers abandoned their calling: 'Their sense of vocation may suffer some blows, but they soldier on despite low pay and dropping attendances.'

Is it any different in the Roman Catholic Church? It is sometimes difficult to discern active evangelisation from within the Catholic fold. The greatest effort towards evangelisation seems to come from a few zealous priests and lay people. However, there are enthusiastic attempts to fan into flame the dwindling embers of a dormant faith particularly in young people. This week I met the youthful NET team from Canada who are in Ireland conducting school retreats. They are brilliant! I am saying this, not just from observation, but from assisting them in the Sacrament of Reconciliation this year and last year. These young evangelists, through mime, song and chat, appear to have an ability to touch the hearts of young Irish boys and girls, scores of whom return to the sacraments after quite a few years. These enthusiasts are assisted in their work by the Catholic Youth Care team in Dublin. As one member of the team said about joining the team, 'I was challenged to stand up for my values, my dignity and most of all my identity as a daughter of God'.

Despite words to the contrary there appears to be little enthusiasm among the hierarchy for direct evangelism. I know of nobody, priest or layperson, being sent for full-time training in the ministry of evangelisation. In our church we prefer our Canon Lawyers to our evangelists! We choose to convert people to a Church rather than to the person of Jesus Christ. The latest fad from on high appears to focus on the liturgy as an instrument of evangelisation, a focus for which it was never intended. We have conveniently forgotten the words of Pope Paul VI who said, 'the Church exists in order to evangelise'.

I admire the wonderful zeal of the Legion of Mary members who are unafraid to proclaim Jesus in a world largely deaf to their message. To be an evangelist demands raw courage and deep faith. To find oneself backed into a corner defending the indefensible rather than proclaiming the infinite love of Jesus has the same impact as an airbag inflating in a crushing accident. One gets bruised! Evangelisation cannot be a solitary ministry. Companionship in faith and love is necessary in this ministry. Have you noticed the passion with which the Young Socialists get involved in every controversy from Dún Laoghaire Baths to Irish Ferries? Even though the day of Socialism has long passed these enthusiasts never flinch. Some of their spirit is needed by those who proclaim another God. Passion for the good news of Jesus is the mark of the true evangelist.

Contemporary Culture and Lapsing from the Faith

We have to ask the question what was the quality of faith in the halcyon days of Irish Catholicism.

It is relatively easy to understand young people not attending Sunday Mass. However, it appears to me that an increasing number of the fifty and sixty years olds are no longer regular churchgoers. These are the people who were reared on the Maynooth Catechism, Sheehan's Apologetics and Hart's Christian Doctrine. For them, the Forty Hours and May Devotions were unmissable. Up to the late 1960s they flocked to St Jude in Whitefriar Street and Miraculous Medal Novena in their local churches. They thronged the annual mission – the first half of the week for women, the second half for men. Bishop Fulton Sheen was the pinup of this generation. Theirs was truly an Irish Catholic culture.

How is it that people who received a sound catechetical training and who were reared in homes steeped in Catholicism have begun to lapse? I have always been surprised by the huge rate of lapsing from the faith among emigrants. Many of these people, when they moved from a social environment where the level of religious practice was over 90 per cent to a culture indifferent to faith, slipped quietly away. Why? Some with a very high level of commitment, like priests and sisters, left the ministry in relatively large numbers. If my observations are correct we have to revisit the halcyon days of Irish Catholicism and ask what was the quality of the faith that appeared so vibrant and so stable.

From my observations, I am less impressed with those who claim that the 'breakdown' of catechetics, or even *Humanae Vitae*, is solely responsible for the secularised culture of today. Would that it were that simple! The process of secularisation arises not just from the loss of faith, but from the loss of social interest in the world of faith. It begins the moment a person feels that religion is irrelevant to the ordinary everyday way of life they are living. It may be that many people today feel that society as such has nothing to do with the truths of faith; it is a different world. I think this is the point at which a growing number of our older people are. They are struggling to make sense of supernatural faith in a foreign land. This is not to deny, however, that a great many of our older parishioners are fervent, prayerful people.

Culture and religion are vitally related. Our present condition is, in my view, partly the outcome of a paradigm shift in Western culture. The Irish Catholic culture of the 1950s and 1960s was unable to adjust to a vibrant, secular culture. Back then the central focus of faith was the Mass. However, there was always a lack of appreciation of the nature and role of liturgy itself. I know that for my late father the Mass was a devotional exercise. The hearts of the people were very engaged with the devotional and it was there that their love, loyalty and faith was nourished. We didn't have an educated, intellectual appreciation of liturgy like English Catholicism had. English Catholicism, with its recusant core, had an intellectual engagement with matters of faith that persists today. The English magazine, *The Tablet*, has for generations drawn lay contributors of a very high calibre. Laudable efforts in this regard were made in Ireland, particularly by the late Basil Clancy and Hibernia, but they petered out.

There was a process of secularisation in the middle of the last millennium – intensified since the eighteenth century – that tried to exclude God and Christianity from all expressions of human life. The Christian religion has been relegated to the confines of each one's private life. Isn't it significant, from this point of view, that all explicit reference to religions was omitted from the European Constitution? This process, which came to Ireland only in the last thirty years or so, is now well advanced. Rather than evangelising the world we are being 'evangelised' by a secular culture. All reference to God, faith and religion has been largely expunged from public life. In such a climate, the retention of a living faith makes far greater demands on the individual Christian.

In a sense, a task of the Church today is the construction of a 'counter-culture', but not of the wagon-train variety. Constructing a counter-culture of faith-based communities open to the world and its possibilities is what I have in mind. We as a Church probably need to realise that it is 'not business as usual'; we are playing on a different stage. Before we played at home; now we are playing away. There is a whole series of questions in relation to faith and practice that we have just ignored or failed to grapple with.

What I am suggesting is a process. The renewal of the Church has to be an organic growth. On a national level there has been no observable discernment by the whole People of God on our current crisis. Would it be possible to have a National Synod? This would give an opportunity to laity and clergy to participate in the restructuring of a church that appears to have lost its way. It is difficult to 'own' an organisation in which one has little influence or power. A National Synod would open up exciting possibilities for wide discernment, practical planning, and perhaps the construction of a National Pastoral Plan for the whole country.

THE DEPTH OF LONELINESS

Loneliness is frightening. There are times when we have to live with the loneliness of mystery.

I was walking along a beach with a friend recently. She asked me, quite spontaneously, 'Do you ever feel lonely?' The question came out of the blue and I struggled to answer. We usually regard loneliness as an enemy. Heartache is not something we invite into our lives. It has become more and more difficult to rest with uneasy feelings. The willingness to be lonely without resolution, when everything in us yearns for something to cheer us up and change our mood, is difficult to come by. When we are lonely we look for a way out. We search for the phone, for companionship, so that we don't have to feel the pain. The Indian poet Tagore wrote, 'Man goes into the noisy crowd to drown his own clamour of silence'. Yet loneliness is a companion to each of us at some time in our lives. The pain of loss and the depth of loneliness when a friend dies can be agonising. I can recall entering a church in the gathering dusk of an autumn evening. From somewhere I heard deep, deep sobbing. As my eyes became accustomed to the diminishing light I saw a little bundle of a man, all alone, crying his heart out. I approached him and asked what was the matter. 'My wife died six months ago,' he told me. 'I just want to die to be with her,' he sobbed. I understood his loneliness. A broken relationship, once full of hope, brings loneliness. American poet Jessica Powers has a beautiful poem, 'There is Homelessness', in which she writes about, 'the homelessness of the soul in the body sown: it is the loneliness of mystery'. I love that phrase, 'the loneliness of mystery'. Our faith journey, when faced, is a journey into the loneliness of mystery. There is a deep pathos about the cry of Jesus on the cross: 'My God, my God, why have you forsaken me?' He experienced the acute loneliness of abandonment. It is so easy to deny our feelings of loneliness. I wonder if the cult of celebrity isn't a frantic chase after attention to quench the possibility of loneliness. I found myself surprised at my reaction to the question I was asked: 'Do you ever feel lonely?'

Some popular musicians have sung about loneliness: Bob Dylan sang, 'How does it feel to be on your own, with no direction home, like a complete unknown, like a rolling stone'; most famously of all, Lennon and McCartney wrote that evocative song 'Eleanor Rigby', with the words, 'all the lonely people, where do they all come from?' They say, 'there is a pill for every ill', but is there a pill for loneliness? Can we 'snap out of it?' I suppose we all wander in a world of desire, which involves looking for alternatives, seeking something to comfort us – food, drink and people. We grope for something because we want to make things be okay.

We can look at loneliness as a problem to be solved, but it's not like that! With an unsolvable problem there are times when we have to rest with the feelings of loneliness. We can experience the depth of loneliness but not as a victim or an object of self-pity. We can ask, 'What are you saying to me, Lord, through this loneliness I am now experiencing?' In a mysterious way the pain of our loneliness can nourish us. If we accept that loneliness is a part of the truth about ourselves at this time, then we can offer that truth up to the Lord. In faith, self-knowledge leads us to a self-acceptance and a self-love that reaches into an awareness of God's love. Because we run from loneliness we frequently fail to learn any lessons from the experience. By acknowledging a painful experience we begin the process of healing because we begin the process of living the truth. This truth, Jesus assures us, will set us free because it is bound up in the ultimate truth that we 'have not here a lasting city'.

It is possible to feel helpless in the face of loneliness, but it doesn't have to be that way. In his book *Man's Search for Meaning*, Victor Frankl has a beautiful passage about a train journey from Auschwitz to a Bavarian camp:

> We beheld the mountains of Salzburg with their summits glowing in the sunset, through the little barred windows of the prison carriage. We were carried away by nature's beauty, which we had missed for so long. In the camp, a man might draw the attention of a comrade next to him to a nice view of the setting sun shining through the tall trees of the Bavarian wood. One evening we were resting on the floor of our hut, dead tired, soup bowls in hand, a fellow prisoner rushed in and asked us to

run out to the assembly ground and see the wonderful sunset. One prisoner said to another; 'how wonderful the world could be'.

The words of St Thérèse come to mind: 'I know that behind the dark cloud my sun is still shinning.' The same is true in loneliness.

Evangelisation is a Strange Word

Catholics have always been uneasy with the word 'evangelisation'. Does it have any practical application to the Church in Ireland?

For the man or woman in the pew, 'evangelisation' is a peculiar word, best used by Protestant Evangelicals of the 'born-again' variety. For some, the word conjures up images of men with sandwich boards that proclaim, 'Repent or you shall all likewise perish'. For others, it is a Billy Graham Rally with people stepping forward to proclaim Jesus as their Saviour. Evangelisation for the ordinary Roman Catholic means being asked, 'Are you saved?' or, worse still, 'When were you saved?' However, the word has now become trendy among professional religious, Catholic and Protestant alike, just as 'going forward' has among business people. We need to find another way of explaining why faith in Christ is a gift 'to be given away'. All other gifts we keep close to ourselves, but the gift of friendship with Jesus is a gift to be shared with others.

The word 'witnessing' also has an evangelical ring about it that most Catholics find disquieting. You might say 'what's in a word?' But words carry emotional undertones accompanied by cultural and traditional baggage that can be off-putting. I looked up my fifty-year-old copy of the Legion of Mary Handbook to discover that the primary object of the Legion of Mary is the 'sanctification of its members by prayer and active co-operation in Mary's and the Church's work of crushing the head of the serpent and advancing the reign of Christ'. The language may be anachronistic and inappropriate for today, but the sentiments are surely still valid. By putting personal sanctification first the Legion was never going to be tempted by a false activism. The Legion also put itself at the disposal of the ecclesiastical authorities, thereby ensuring that any work it did was 'at the heart of the Church'. 'The head of the serpent' is hardly a particularly sensitive expression, but we are in a spiritual warfare and there are many voices thoroughly hostile to the Gospel.

The word 'evangelisation' comes to us from ancient history when a slave was chosen to bring back to the ruler the good news of victory in battle. The bearer of this good news was always granted his freedom and so he would come running, even dancing for joy, as he brought home the news of victory that would gain him his freedom. Christianity burst on the world with all the suddenness of good news: good news proclaimed with great enthusiasm and courage by its advocates, and backed by their own conviction that God had transformed the apparent defeat of Good Friday into the victory of Easter Sunday.

Jesus read from Isaiah, 'the Spirit of the Lord is upon me, because he has anointed me to preach the good news to the poor'. We can easily forget that we too have been anointed for the same task. Through our Baptism and Confirmation we have received the anointing that allows us to share in the priesthood of Christ. That gives us the task of sharing the good news of what Jesus did for us according to our ability. The good news is hardly news in the ordinary sense of the word. Jesus is the good news. It is hard to introduce someone to a person you yourself have never met! To tell others, one must know Jesus oneself. So the good news is truly personal. It is attempting to introduce others, in whatever way is appropriate, to the person of Jesus. Christianity, in the beginning, was a lay movement and the news of it was spread by ordinary people. At the start the infectious enthusiasm on the part of different people of different backgrounds, sex and cultures was backed up, for the most part, by the quality of their lives. Their love, their joy, their changed habits and transformed characters gave great weight to what they had to say. Their community lives were sufficiently different to attract notice, to invite curiosity and to inspire and motivate others to follow in their footsteps. Paganism saw in early Christianity a quality of living and of dying that could not be found elsewhere. Someone once said, 'the heart of the problem is the human heart'. Could it be that the starting point for each of us begins, not in changing structures, but in changing ourselves?

FANORE SUMMER CAMP
– A SPIRITUAL EXPERIENCE

For thirty years a summer camp has taken place near
the stony Burren limestone at Fanore. For many it is
an oasis of peace in a busy world.

Fanore is no Waikiki Beach! But it is unique in its awesome
scenery, and in its annual Christian Summer Camp for young
people. Beneath the spectacular stony grey limestone of the
Burren, for the past thirty years, teenagers and twentysomethings,
some with their parents, gather for an exceptional week of prayer,
play and praise. The man behind this event is Fr Peter Casey, the
Parish Priest of Ballinaigh in the Kilmore Diocese. Peter, in tee
shirt, jeans, baseball cap and bare feet, although fifty-seven years
of age, could fit snugly into a beach volley-ball team or a rugby
scrum. Tall, broad shouldered and still enthusiastic after all these
years, he is the pivotal man behind this extraordinary enterprise.

'In 1976 I was working in a Vocational School in Kilmore
and I brought a crowd of young people down here. We were
joined by a group from Lucan and Limerick. We had nothing.
A few tatty tents and our desire to grow in our relationship with
God was about all we had. It was tough back then,' he said ruefully.

'There was physical hardship and a lot of sacrifice,' he continued. Thirty years later, the sons and daughters of those early pioneers are packing them in once more at Fanore beach in Co. Clare. For instance, I met former schoolteacher Bernadine Callery, now studying for a Masters degree at DCU, who was participating in her nineteenth summer camp. 'I feel spiritually deprived if I don't come,' she told me. Then there was Ronan McCann, a solicitor, based in Manchester, who came with his fiancée Lisa. 'It gives me strength for the year,' he said. 'My parents had a real experience of God here many years ago. I have been coming for twenty years. I wouldn't miss it for anything,' he continued laughingly. His brother Peter, once a professional footballer with Blackburn Rovers, is a deeply committed Christian who has given his life to the work of evangelisation, especially with athletes. 'This is a most powerful place for me,' he said. 'I have also been coming here for twenty years.' Marty Timlin and his wife Julie came with their two children. This is their eleventh visit. 'I find fellowship and spiritual refreshment here every year.'

The daily schedule at Fanore includes a Morning Prayer meeting and Exposition of the Blessed Sacrament. Football, swimming and fun take place in the afternoon. Daily Mass is at 8 p.m. This is no ordinary Mass! When I visited during the week the Mass lasted nearly two hours! It was full of participation accompanied by the gentle noise of Atlantic breakers in the background. The singing, led by a great music group, was loud and enthusiastic. Silent prayer for an hour is at night from 11 p.m. to midnight.

Peter is at great pains to emphasise the extraordinary help and hospitality the Camp has experienced from the local

McCormack family who own the site at Fanore. 'Joe and Lily, and now their sons, have facilitated us in every way. They have been wonderful,' Peter told me. For the camp he bought a large marquee-type building which is sited in the dunes and is stored locally during the year. A battered bus, painted a gaudy purple, is headquarters and accommodation for Fr Peter. The participants hire out the mobile homes that scatter the shore line. Everyone looks after their own needs. Mike and Ann Loughman, both teachers in Dublin, were here with their son Hugh and have been coming annually with their children. Ann said that the camp was a spiritual pick-me-up with a wonderful sense of community.

Andrea Roeder-Bubel from Germany is on her twelfth visit. 'I came as a tourist to the area and just happened to notice all the young people going to Mass, so I joined them. It was all an accident really!' She is now a full-time pastoral worker in her own parish in Germany. Nadine Rosen and her boyfriend David Goeller, from near Heidelberg, were invited to come by Andrea. David is studying music and is about to enter his final year at university. 'I come because I find peace and healing here,' he said.

A visit to this unique camp restored my hope and faith in young people. Their *joie de vivre* left me in buoyant mood as I returned home. We were meant to live our Christian lives in community. We need one another. In Fanore one experiences solidarity in faith, community living, prayer and praise. But above all it is fun! Trekking in the Burren, swimming at Fanore and fishing in the wild Atlantic are as much part of this summer camp as the prayer. The happy faces tell the story!

Fire in the Belly

We are driven by desire. Without a fire within we will not have a passion for spreading the wonderful news of our salvation.

In his book *The Holy Longing*, Ronald Rolheiser writes, 'we are forever restless, dissatisfied, frustrated and aching. We are so overcharged with desire that it is hard to come to simple rest. There is a fundamental dis-ease within'. The centrality of desire in the make-up of the human person is for the most part unacknowledged. Obsessional desire to achieve is a perplexing drive. Yet without this 'fire in the belly' to make things different, for myself or others, the human person seems anaemic, listless and disinteresting.

In May 1992 Deepak Kulkarni attempted to climb Everest as part of an Indian expedition. His frozen corpse, clipped to fixed ropes, hangs on the South Col of Everest, an indifferent object to future climbers. A Japanese woman, Yasuko Namba, also lies abandoned on Everest. In the rush to get to the top, many climbers now simply pass dead bodies, their desire to get to the summit conquering all other instincts.

Journalist Paul Kimmage, wrote of his relationship with his girlfriend Ann: 'Our relationship was three years old and we were totally committed to each other, but my obsession with cycling made it impossible to plan anything.'

When John Ridgeway was asked why he rowed across the Atlantic in 1966 he replied, 'Because afterwards, when I come into a room, people will say there is the man who rowed the Atlantic.' It was desire that led Issac Jogues, an early Jesuit, to be butchered to death by the Mohawk Indians of Northern Canada in 1646. Look at the fire in the belly of Bob Geldof who drove Live Aid to the relief of the 1985 Ethiopian famine?

Without that fire nothing on such a grand scale could have happened. What do we do with our longings? Dream on, or take one small step to make things different? Rolheiser claims that 'spirituality is about what we do with our longings, our unrest, our dis-ease'. Evangelical Christians often display a manic intensity about their witnessing that may be driven by a desire to convert people to Christ. Desire in the spiritual realm invariably rests in a confused potpourri of motives that are difficult to disentangle. Yet it was Jesus who lit the fire of desire in the human person when he said to the first disciples, 'Go therefore teach all nations …'.

The Church always had a difficulty about a desire that drove people to give everything for Christ. It spoke about avoiding singularity. Anything that drew attention to the self was to be shunned. Humility was a virtue that almost quenched the fire within. There was no gutsy ambition about our notion of spirituality. I have wondered at the success of people who left the active ministry. Sometimes it seems that their talents only fully flowered when they left. Perhaps the fire within was stifled by an anaemic spirituality that failed to cater for the robustness of youthful desire. The Spanish mystic, John of the Cross, begins his famous treatment on the soul's journey with the words: 'One dark night, fired with love's urgent longings ... I went out unseen, my house being now all stilled.' What a breathtaking phrase, 'fired with love's urgent longings'! We must not end up dispirited, jaded, wearied and worn down, but excited about following 'love's urgent longings'.

Controversies have their place in the village square, but remember that in the eye of the storm is the tranquillity of knowing one is loved. The desire to respond to love is the turbine that powers the apostolate. 'Being nice to people', laudable as it is, is not a spirituality of desire that will make things happen. Something more is needed. It is remarkable that people of passion, often with disordered lives, become great people of God – St Paul, Matt Talbot, Charles de Foucauld, St Augustine, Dorothy Day, Thomas Merton and others. The fire within these people was not tamed but redirected and poured out for God and others. The fire in the belly needs to be fuelled by drawing closer to its source. It is sustained in community. It breaks out in unconditional love. Hold fast to dreams, for if dreams die life is a broken-winged bird that cannot fly.

Forgiveness is Healing

Lack of forgiveness holds two people in bondage. How can we pray the Lord's Prayer and hold bitterness in our heart?

I don't often cry. But I can well remember that May day in 1994 feeling the warmth of my tears as they trickled down my face. I was watching the inaugural address of Nelson Mandela on television. Erect, proud, but above all forgiving were the impressions he made on me. Recently released, after a horrible thirty years in jail, this is what he said:

> The time for healing has come.
> The moment to bridge the chasms that divide us has come.
> The time to build is upon us.
> We have triumphed in the efforts to implant hope in the breasts of the millions of our people. We enter into a covenant that we shall build the society in which all South Africans, both black and white, will be able to walk tall, without any fear in their

hearts, assured of their inalienable right to human dignity – a rainbow nation at peace with itself and the world.

There was another time I cried. That was when I heard the extraordinary words of forgiveness on the lips of Gordon Wilson after the horrible Provisional IRA bombing at Enniskillen. His beautiful daughter Marie had been brutally snatched from him. Among his first words were ones of forgiveness for her murderers and a pledge of daily prayers on their behalf. What a man!

There is another incident of great forgiveness in recent years. Pope John Paul slumped forward in his limousine rocked by the bullets of Mehet Ali Agca. It was 13 May 1981. After his recovery and recuperation, among his first visits was to the Regina Coeli jail in Rome to offer forgiveness to his potential assassin.

There is something noble about forgiveness. As I was typing this reflection a man rang up. 'What are you doing', he asked. 'I am writing a reflection on forgiveness,' I replied sheepishly. His reply was immediate: 'Sure, if we don't forgive we die.' Wisdom comes from unexpected quarters.

Against the tapestry of these recent incidents we hear the words 'Father, forgive them for they know what they do' echoing from the cross. Jesus walked through the threshold of forgiveness before us.

Where there is lack of forgiveness two people are in bondage. One closes the door on the inside denying access to the other. The other cannot enter the bolted door. Lack of forgiveness is like a cancer. It involves a playing and replaying of real or supposed hurts. It festers and intensifies as long as the hand of forgiveness is withheld. How can we change our heart if it is filled with bitterness and lack of forgiveness? I think I know! Praying sincerely for the person who has hurt you and wishing for them all God wishes for him or her often produces dramatic results. It is so hard to pray for a person and at the same time harbour bitterness and resentment.

The Lord's Prayer is frightening. When Robert Louis Stevenson the author of *Treasure Island* lived in the South Sea Islands he used to conduct family worship in the mornings for his household. It always concluded with the Lord's Prayer. One morning in the middle of the Lord's Prayer he rose from his knees and left the room. His health was always precarious, so his wife followed him thinking that he was ill. 'Is there anything wrong?' she asked. 'Only this,' said Stevenson, 'I am not fit to pray the Lord's Prayer today.' No one is fit to pray the Lord's Prayer so long as the unforgiving spirit holds sway within his heart. If a man has not put things right with others, he cannot put things right with God.

In this great prayer we ask God to forgive us in proportion and to the extent that we forgive others. Forgiveness is healing. I can recall preaching about forgiveness at a prayer meeting about twenty years ago. I thought nothing of it until a woman approached me the following week. 'You preached about forgiveness last week,' she said. 'I did,' I replied. 'I was moved by your sermon.' She explained. 'I have a brother in Australia with whom I hadn't spoken for eleven years. We fell out over a family quarrel. Last week after the meeting I went home determined to ring my brother. Imagine my great joy when he answered the phone and broke down at the prospect of reconciliation. We talked and talked for ages and he is planning to visit me in Ireland next year. I am so happy.' What a wonderful healing.

THE GRIP OF THE CHURCH LOOSENS IN SPAIN

The recent history of Spain parallels what has been happening in Ireland for the last twenty years.

On 20 November 1975, Spanish Dictator General Franco, '*El Caudillo*', died in hospital of natural causes. At the time I was holidaying in the Canary Islands. It was the beginning of a long Good Friday. Everything closed down. The conversation among holiday makers was whether they would be able to get a flight home or not. Levity was discouraged. The eerie, sombre atmosphere that hung over the Islands reminded me of a Belfast Sunday in the 1960s. 'What will happen now?' people wondered in whispers. Here was a man who had won a vicious civil war, who had forged an intimate alliance with the Roman Catholic Church called National Catholicism and whose death most people thought would reopen wounds too deep to heal. At the moment I am reading *Ghosts of Spain: Travels through a Country's Hidden Past* by *Guardian* journalist Giles Tremlett. What intrigues me is not the excellence of the book, but rather how the history of Spain, since Franco's death, parallels what has been happening in Ireland in the last two decades. As in Ireland, the

Church was a constant chaperone for Spaniard's private lives. In 1958 the Spanish Bishops' Conference warned that unmarried couples who promenaded arm-in-arm were placing themselves in '*periculo grave*' (grave danger)! Schooling was largely in the hands of Church-run institutions. Much of the social services and health care was the preserve of the Church. Not any more. While the bishops huff and puff, the gulf between the teaching of the Church and what Spaniards want to do continues to widen. Mass attendance has plummeted. Divorce was legalised in 1981. Abortion is now available almost on demand; so much so that British women are now travelling to Spain for late-term abortions. This is a reversal of the once traditional traffic of young Spanish women travelling to London. Spaniards seem now as deaf to the Vatican as the Irish. The grip of the Church on Spanish life has been loosened to such an extent that Prime Minister Jose Luis Rodriguez Zapatero felt confident enough to extend equal rights to gays and transvestites. Spain became the third country in the world to introduce gay marriage.

Recently I had a brief opportunity to experience Church life in Spain first hand. How was the Counter Reformation being conducted? I attended two Masses at the Parish of San Millan, Seggovia. On both occasions the congregations were well into the sixty-plus age group. A sprinkling of young people tried, in a desultory fashion, to encourage some congregational singing at the second Mass. The elderly priest preached ad nauseam. However, the parish newsletter contained a very firmly worded statement from Julio Alonso Arranz, the local bishop, saying that in future no child who failed to undergo a three-year catechetical preparation would be permitted to receive his or her First Holy

Communion. All aspects of what was expected were outlined in detail.

The Sunday previous I attended a Confirmation ceremony in Parroquia La Purisima in Salamanca. Here the minimum age for Confirmation is eighteen! Twelve young women and five young men, aged between eighteen and twenty-two, were being confirmed by local bishop Carlos Lopez. Catechist Gerardo Bueno, a lawyer, explained to me that each person must request the Sacrament and be prepared to undergo an intensive two-year catechetical programme. Then the individual must put their request in writing for the consideration of the parish priest, Jose Manuel Hernandez, and the bishop. They are expected to give their reasons for requesting the sacrament. The parish priest emphasised that 'the community supports these young people on their journey'. At the beginning of the ceremony the two catechists spoke to the congregation saying that they were satisfied the young people had prepared diligently for the Sacrament and in their opinion were suitable candidates for Confirmation. I asked the crucial question! Knowing that in Ireland Confirmation is the exit door from Church life, I asked if those confirmed would persevere in the faith. Bueno informed me with confidence that 80 per cent of those who are confirmed will persevere. In fact, they will now become involved in the life of the parish and in the many small apostolic groups that are established here'. If only the Church in Ireland had even a fraction of such initiative!

The Hard Road to Klondike

One hundred and sixty years ago Ireland was a different place! Michael MacGowan looks with longing on the neighbourliness and charity of that time.

Many years ago I read a book that enthralled me. Come what may, I intended to hold on to it. But alas, I either lent it and it wasn't returned, or I lost it in one of my many moves. Anyway, this book, *The Hard Road to Klondike* by Michael MacGowan, has been reprinted. The book falls very much into the Blasket Island genre of reminiscences. Michael, from near Gortahork in Donegal, was born in 1865 and was hired out to a farmer at a 'hiring fair' in Letterkenny when only nine years of age. He had little English. For six successive summers he was hired out for varying periods. Then he went thinning turnips in Scotland. Eventually, in the 1890s, he ended up as a participant in that crazy, cruel, gold rush to the Klondike in the frozen north of Canada.

We can look back at our past with rose-coloured spectacles; better still we can learn from the past. Michael captures an Ireland that some believe holds the key today to whether we are an economy or a society. 'The people of this area,' he wrote, 'were as poor as could be. They had no land worth talking about and it was hard to make any kind of a living out of the bits of soil between the rocks. But there was one gift the people had: there was friendship and charity among them; they helped one another in work and in trouble, in adversity and in pain, and it was that neighbourliness which, with the grace of God, was the solid stanchion of their lives.'

Where is the glue that holds our society together today? Rushing from bed, to crèche, to work, to shopping mall, to ballet class, to pub, to home, to bed, rips what Michael calls the 'stanchion' or foundation of our lives asunder. Even when there was fever in the home of two parents and ten children, Peggy Mor of the Rosses, who was 'knowledgeable about curing fevers', was sent for and 'she came straight away and gave my mother every help while we were on the flat of our backs'. This isn't nostalgic pathos! Here we have enduring virtues of charity and neighbourliness worked out in practical action. What treasurers we have lost, or thrown away, in our pell-mell rush to the trough of success! When Michael got severe frostbite on the Klondike and it looked as if his end was near, he wrote: 'I never felt as deserted as I did then. I had great faith and hope in God at the same time, and I never prayed hard to Him in my life that He didn't answer me. People don't know the miracles that God can work until they're in real trouble and what saved me that morning in my affliction was one of God's miracles.' If Ireland has abandoned the faith is it 'good riddance' or an incalculable loss that future generations will regret?

How can we take the spiritual riches of the past and maintain them in our rush for more and more prosperity. Kindness, care

MARTIN TIERNEY

for the weak, sharing what we have, strengthening the family, are not values hostile to prosperity. In the 'time poverty' of the present, our need is to integrate these values into a way of living that still allows us to prosper. My mother used to say 'much wants more!' When money owns us, rather than we owning money, we turn spiritual values upside down and the pursuit of wealth becomes single-minded. If this happens what will we have to show for it all? How will our children remember us? Why not try to write your own obituary through the eyes of another. Such an exercise could help one determine where we stand in terms of values.

HEALING THE PAIN

We cannot move on as a Church until we have dealt with the scandals of clerical sex abuse. Entering into the darkness and fearlessly seeking the truth is critical to future healing.

Some might be tempted to think that this has been an *annus horribilis* for the Church in Ireland. I am not so sure. It could, but need not be, the worst year ever. If we as a Church begin to know more clearly both the integrity and brokenness of our motivation; if we can sense more realistically our duplicity, we can become more aware of our goodness and see more sharply our values and priorities. If we become more open to seeing ourselves as we are, as a Church – if we desire to see ourselves as God sees us – things can happen; and if we can recognise the Divine working within the Church, then there can be growth.

As well as personal self-knowledge, there is a need for us to reflect on ourselves as Church, rather than as individuals who happen to be members of this Church. A lot depends on our willingness to face up to our own darkness. I have heard bishop after bishop say 'sorry' for clerical sex abuse. I need to hear more.

I need to hear the issues of secrecy and abuse of authority being dealt with in an open and frank way. That hasn't happened yet. Blaming others can be a sterile business. To blame the abusers, the bishops, the media for our troubles can be personally comforting. However, I have a need to look into my own soul to discover there my complicity in the failure of the Church to be the salt of the earth and the light of the world. St Teresa of Avila wrote, 'the path of self-knowledge must never be abandoned, nor is there on this journey a soul so much a giant that it has no need to return often to the stage of an infant and a suckling'. She goes on to say in the Book of Her Life that 'self knowledge and the thought of one's sins is the bread with which all palates must be fed no matter how delicate they may be'.

Rather than lamenting what has happened in recent years, or perhaps even asking why it has happened, would it not be more fruitful to ask what the Lord is saying to us as individuals and as a Church through these happenings? God speaks to us through the circumstances of our daily lives. In a mysterious way we can be nourished by our own evil if we accept that evil as a part of the truth about ourselves. In other words we need to listen to the voice of the Spirit speaking to us through the pain. If we keep finding excuses or blaming others, we drive up a cul-de-sac and hear the echo of our own voices. Thérèse of Lisieux wrote in her collected Letter that 'Jesus delights to teach her, as He taught St Paul, the science of glorying in one's infirmities'. Self-knowledge leads us to an awareness of both our evil and God's strength. Have we faced our own evil? I would love to see the Church engaging in an honest, sincere examination of conscience. Have we dug holes too deep with our personal prejudices to allow this to happen? When we find ourselves not listening to our total experience or excluding part of it, or evaluating it according to our own expectations, we cannot expect progress. When we dissect rather than receive, when we make our reflections ethical considerations of what should be rather than faith-awareness of what is, or when we manipulate our reflections by refusing to enter into certain areas, then we have limited the possibilities of finding God's word in our experiences.

I have heard people referring to our present trials as 'a purification'. This may be true. What then are the ethical and religious implications of this purification? People have also talked of a humbler Church of the future. Again this may be true. What are the practical implication of evidencing this humility in the day-to-day life of the Church?

I feel a little uneasy that we are not learning from the experiences of the past. Everyone, priest and lay person, is left to make their own sense of what has happened. I am not sure if that is good enough. This is where we need our bishops to reflect with us on the way forward in the light of the Gospel. We have to pick ourselves up and dust ourselves off, and follow the star of God's goodness. In acknowledging a painful experience, we begin the process of healing, because we begin the process of living the truth. We owe this to the victims of clerical sex abuse. Any compensation they deservedly receive will never heal the scars. A renewed Church is God's gift. We can embrace our experiences as a death leading to a little resurrection.

Inviting Back Inactive Catholics

We say that the Church is a family, a community of sorts. If this is so why are we so uncaring towards those who leave?

For John, cutting himself off from the Catholic Church was a sudden decision. John is gay and the Roman Catholic Church is not a safe haven for gay people. He had had enough. He had a sense that the Catholic Church just did not respect the dignity of homosexual people. He would find a place where he was respected. He left vowing never to return.

For Gill, receiving the Eucharist has no particular significance: 'It's just something I do wherever I go to Mass which isn't very often.'

Mike rebelled because of sexuality. 'Catholics are supposed to be abstinent until marriage. I don't believe in abstinence; I do believe in sex before marriage.'

David is fifty-eight, married, a father of five and until quite recently was a practising Catholic. 'I didn't find the Church credible any more. I wasn't hearing answers to the questions that troubled me. I just didn't feel part of the Church and I certainly hadn't any possibility of influencing it. At least as a citizen I can vote. I have some say. The sky didn't fall in when I stopped going.'

Jane said: 'My friends don't go to Mass but they consider themselves believers. I don't go to Mass on Sundays. I only go on important occasions. I cannot speak badly of the Church as an institution because I've only met good people.'

Peter told me: 'I bring my mother to Lourdes every year but I have left the Church. All the clerical sex abuse scandals made me question everything. I just couldn't be bothered having anything to do with the Church any more.'

These are real people. They live in ordinary houses in your street, avenue or road. They went to Catholic schools. They made their First Communion and First Confession. Some of them married in church. At one time a few seriously thought of becoming a priest or religious. Now, however, they have cut the umbilical cord with the community that we call Church. The life of the Church no longer affects how they live their lives. The memories of their church-going days are beginning to ebb away. They still go to funerals and weddings, but as spectators rather than participators. They remain untouched.

How would you feel if your brother, sister, father or mother got up from the kitchen table and walked out the door saying, 'I am leaving this family. I am fed up with all of you. Just forget about me – I'm gone'? Think about what you would do! Every year we have missing people and extraordinary efforts are made to seek the return of the lost. Posters go into shop windows and onto lamp posts. Radio appeals are made and friends scour the countryside. Re-enactments are played out to try to jog people's memories. Nothing is too much trouble. The anguish of the next-of-kin is traumatic. If one is to judge by the negligible efforts made by the Catholic Church to look for the lost and bring back the strayed one would think that the Church just couldn't care less. Or could it be that we have a Church that we don't believe in enough to care about those who have left?

We all can tell our story – why we are Catholic and intend to remain so. We can speak of the influence of God in the cares, troubles and joys of life. We can talk about the gift the Eucharist is to each of us on our journey. We can pray and praise the God who loves each person (whether active in the Church or not) more than we could ever dream of. All this is true. But the path of the evangelist is a lonely one. We need the support of the like-minded. This article was prompted by a brief visit to the website of CASE, the English Catholic Bishop's agency for evangelisation. I was impressed with a Church that does care enough to seek out those in need. I was impressed with the strategies for evangelisation. I was buoyed up by the fresh ideas and enthusiasm of the agency's staff. I was saddened that the Church in Ireland just doesn't seem to care enough to do anything positive to invite those who have left to 'return home'.

THE LONELINESS OF
LOVELESS SEX

*Sex sells everything, but Dawn Eden discovered to her
shame that it didn't bring the happiness she longed for.*

I read an article in the *Sunday Times* that intrigued me. It was
about a promiscuous thirtysomething whose life was empty and
filled with longing. For years she used sex in the vain hope that
she would find that someone special who would fulfil all her
needs. She went on a spiral of 'meet a guy who attracts, have sex,
dump or be dumped, end up unhappy' and begin all over again.
Her frenetic sexual activity left her bleak and lonely. The
inevitability of the recurring cycle imprisoned her.

Sex is frightening in what it promises to many young people
and in what it fails to deliver. But sex sells – everything from cars
to cosmetics, from detergents to stair carpets. It is sexy smut that
fuels comedians, television shows and teenage magazines. It
holds out the hope of winning the 'happiness lotto' every day. It
gathers young people into its vortex and spews many out
disillusioned. Watch the 'me generation' teen queue up on a
Saturday night to get into a disco in south Dublin – or anywhere
in modern Ireland, from Ballina to Dingle. The skimpy clothes

they are wearing are probably not those in which they left home. They probably hid them from their parents and changed into them on the way to the disco. They are walking advertisements for availability. For the boys to 'pull' a girl is the focus of the night. Please excuse the language, but one website claimed that this disco 'was the place to go to get laid'! It isn't easy to face this reality. Motivated by status, peer pressure, loneliness and lust, or not wanting to be a wallflower, the testosterone is unrestrained. I have baptised children, the mothers of whom had no idea even of the name of the father – the fruit of a one-night-stand in a dark, alcohol-fuelled haze. Sex is not just the fruit of a relationship any more; it is a commodity with which to sell everything. The message is that without an active sex life you are as awkward as a ghost in a graveyard. Lust, we are told, is a way station on the road to love. It isn't. The question of morality, right and wrong, appears irrelevant. In this context the concept of sin, in the strictly religious meaning, is as confusing as speaking Swahili in Red Square.

Parents, or grandparents, some advice: beg, borrow or buy Dawn Eden's book *The Thrill of the Chaste: Finding Fulfilment while Keeping your Clothes On*! This is a book that you can give to the needy young person whose welfare is closest to your heart. Eden writes, 'I sacrificed what should have been the best years of my life for the black lie of free love. All the sex I ever had – and I had more than my fair share – far from bringing me the lasting relationship I sought, only made marriage a more distant prospect'.

Eden's conversion was surprisingly providential. As a journalist she was doing a phone interview with Ben Eshbach, the leader of a Los Angeles rock band. She asked him what he was reading. His answer was G.K. Chesterton's *The Man who was Thursday*. She got the book and was soon reading everything by Chesterton, captivated by his defence and passionate advocacy of Christianity. She (a lapsed Jew) continued her dissipated lifestyle until one day, 'I got on my knees and prayed – and eventually entered the Catholic Church' (this is making a long story very short!). She claims that she was looking for love in all the wrong places.

Pure In Heart is a growing Dublin-based youth community dedicated to living the true beauty of sexuality. They believe that sexuality is a gift to be treasured and respected, finding its full expression in marriage. The young people in this group believe that they are truly free to be the people they are created to be, to love properly with their bodies. This is the virtue of chastity. It is too easy to brand all young people with the promiscuous label. The young people in the Pure In Heart community give workshops in schools and to community groups. In a non-judgemental atmosphere their mission is to promote the idea of chastity before marriage. They can be contacted at ask@pureinheart.net

Love and Marriage

Love has become a word contaminated by a culture
where 'looking after number one' is so important. Love
is not a feeling but a decision.

In *Oliver!*, the musical version of Charles Dickens' book *Oliver Twist*, the poor, orphaned Oliver is sold to an undertaker and his family. Roughly treated, the young boy is forced to sleep in the basement among the coffins in the undertaker's shop. He is alone and thoroughly depressed. He begins to sing:

> Where is love?
> Does it fall from the skies above?
> Is it underneath the willow tree
> that I've been dreaming of?
> Must I travel far and wide
> 'til I am beside the someone who
> I can mean something to?

We all need to be 'special' to someone else. To be 'special' in the life of another is to experience that person as 'the bread of life'.

Such a person nourishes your life. Marriage is a mystery. Two people, who at one time were complete strangers to one another, fall in love and enter the most intimate of unions that it is possible for human beings to have. I find it almost impossible to believe that the finger of God is absent from such a coming together.

Real intimacy is neither instant nor temporary. Loyalty is the quality that makes friendships endure. A true and loyal friend is a treasure. People go to 'singles bars' and go on 'singles holidays' is search of enduring friendship. They go because they believe in the value of friendship and wish with all their hearts to find it.

About five years ago a body was pulled from the River Liffey. For over a week the corpse lay unidentified in the city morgue. I recall at the time experiencing a deep sadness that this person, even in death, had no one to claim him. Was he special to no one? Later he was identified only through the spectacles he wore. How terribly sad!

The history of David and Jonathan is one of history's best-known friendships. It is a story of the mystery of friendship's beginning and the irresistible loyalty it engenders. Jonathan's soul became closely bound to David's and Jonathan came to love him as his own soul. Jonathan made a pact with David to love him as his own soul; he took off the cloak he was wearing and gave it to David, and his armour too, even his sword, his bow and his belt (1 Sam 18).

I deal with the word 'love' at arm's length and I view it with a jaundiced eye! I am reluctant to use the word. I dislike it because it has become a counterfeit word disguising the reality of its beauty behind an ersatz smarm. I have an aversion to the word because millions of young people are buying into a notion of

MARTIN TIERNEY

love than begins with the self. Self-fulfilment can become the pinnacle of our ambitions. But it is in the beloved, 'the other' that happiness is found. No one person can totally fulfil the needs of another, but we are told that 'love' can! It has become overly identified with sexuality. What certain magazines are fond of calling 'recreational sex' is sometimes confused with love.

This general confusion about love has seeped into marriage. There was a time when glossy magazines ran articles asking, 'Can this Marriage be Saved?', and the answer was usually, 'Yes'. Today, however, public opinion seems to have reversed itself. The same magazines now ask, 'Should this Marriage be Saved?', and they are inclined to answer, 'No'.

It is not that long ago since the action of a rapist was described in a Dublin court as 'making love'. Is this an indication that sexual intercourse has become identified with love? More often than not sex education today is little more than a lesson in the biological mechanics of intercourse. This is a necessary beginning but hardly a substitute for the beauty of a committed relationship for life. I dislike the word 'love' because it is depicted only as 'that warm feeling inside' and little else. The way the word 'love' is used and misunderstood almost makes it an inappropriate word to apply to God.

If the word 'love' was understood, would so many marriages be breaking up? If young people knew that real love equals 'tough love', would they become disenchanted quite so quickly? The stability of marriage is pivotal for both the well-being of the Church and of society.

In Thornton Wilder's *The Skin of Our Teeth*, Mrs Antrobus says to her husband:

I didn't marry you because you were perfect, George. I didn't even marry you because I loved you. I married you because you gave me a promise. That promise made up for your faults. And the promise I gave you made up for mine. Two imperfect people got married and it was the promise that made the marriage.

Love to be sure is an emotion and a feeling and of course it includes a powerful sexual attraction. Love that lasts is this and much more. It also is a decision. The feelings that are part of love may wax and wane over the years. The decision to love is rooted far deeper in the heart. The Church teaches that marriage is forever, and the marital promise is meant to be kept. It is the decision to love, irrespective of the feelings of the moment, that will keep a marriage alive.

The Married Single Lifestyle

There are times when partners in a marriage in pain cope with their difficulties by living 'a married single lifestyle'.

When couples begin to share feelings, they begin to become friends, not just spouses or lovers. This element of friendship is mentioned frequently by couples in good relationships. I love to hear a husband or wife describe their life partner as 'my best friend' and say, 'we can talk about anything'. Sadly, because some marriages begin with a sexual attraction rather than friendship, some couples never become really good friends. Couples in difficulty will say, 'We have talked until the cows come home but we are no nearer resolving our problems'. So often it is that the husband talks out of his head, the woman responds from the heart and they become like two railway tracks always in parallel, never together. It is only when they begin to communicate from the same point, namely their feelings, that true dialogue begins.

Being a friend means being able to share ideas, activities and feelings without being owned or judged. There is reluctance on the part of so many young people today to cross the line from a dating relationship into the permanency of marriage. Traditional courtship patterns are being short-circuited. Many relationships move quickly from being an acquaintance to being a lover. The 'getting to know you' process is overtaken by raging hormones. Many married couples today are, in fact, 'married singles'. To be a married single is to lead a single life in all but name under the same roof as someone else.

I received a letter from a reader who revealed the loneliness found within many marriages. With her permission I share her thoughts.

> I am a fifty-two-year-old woman, married now for almost thirty-three years and the mother of four grown-up children. I am wondering if I am one of a kind or if there are more women like myself who are married and yet feel 'unmarried'. I do not want to be divorced nor do I want an affair. I feel very lonely, unloved, unappreciated and just seen 'to be there' – desperate for a loving, caring companion. I'm too old for the jet set and too young for the senior citizen category.

Believe me, the married single lifestyle is increasingly becoming the norm rather than the exception. In a relationship when 'my needs' or 'my fulfilment' become the prime motivating force of the relationship it is time for a serious examination, a marriage check-up. Sport, socialising or work can draw a person out of the home like an enticing magnet. Until our society begins to consider 'workaholism' as equal in its destructive force on a

MARTIN TIERNEY

marriage as other more recognisable addictions, married couples will be drawn into the married single lifestyle, which ultimately leads to a sterile old age and perhaps a marriage in tatters. A person can also become so wrapped up in their offspring that they have little time for their spouse. So-called laudable activities can draw them away from their spouse into a single lifestyle.

Thousands of 'unmarried' married people in the world are lonely. For reasons of their own, they choose to remain in a relationship that began with love but deteriorated through the years. Research has shown that men need women more than women need men, because women are usually intimacy-givers while men tend to be intimacy-takers.

Even within couples that develop friendship, life is not always smooth because one may not enjoy what the other enjoys. When this happens couples try to change one another. Never forget, in the last analysis, there is only one person you can change – that is yourself! When couples go down the road of blame it can compound the hurt and open new wounds. You cannot unspill spilled milk! If both decide to change then the rehabilitation of a relationship has already begun. I believe that the change can only come when both are willing to reveal their true feelings without fear of scolding, judgement or penalties. Each must be willing to recognise that they too have contributed to the breakdown of the relationship, just as they have a major part to play in its rehabilitation.

Don't forget that feelings are neither right nor wrong – they just are. It is only when we react out of feelings that we enter the area of ethics or morality. We can feel sad, angry, upset, lonely or disappointed. We have a right to our feelings; they are not there

as material for judgement but to become the stuff of
understanding.

> When I ask you to listen to me
> and you start giving advice
> you have not done what I have asked.

> When I ask you to listen to me
> and you begin to tell me why I shouldn't feel that
> way
> you are trampling on my feelings.

MARTIN TIERNEY

MISSING PERSONS

Monitoring the use of the internet has become one more important chore that parents have to undertake. Not to do so can lead to tragic unforeseen family difficulties.

On Tuesday 3 April this year, fifteen year old Samantha Osborn from Buckingham disappeared. Her father and mother 'had some words with her' about her use of the internet. Samantha stormed out the front door with only the clothes on her back and hasn't been seen since. Ironically, the very tool that may assist in returning her to her parents and the family home may have led to her disappearance. Increasingly young people are meeting, not in cafes, the local park or the bowling alley, but in cyberspace. The Osborns suspect that Samantha met someone on the internet, perhaps an older person, and vanished! With the help of their thirteen-year-old son, a computer wizard, they have managed to contact most of the people Samantha was talking to in cyberspace, but without advancing the possibility of having her home again.

In Britain, 75 per cent of all young people between 18 and 24 years use social networking sites. It is unlikely that it is much different here. Websites such as Facebook, Myspace and Bebo have created a place of gathering, a polyglot, a forum, for young people to connect, converse or just 'chill out'. No longer is it necessary for them to meet face to face, or even to be sure to whom they are talking. It's all in the ether! This is good but like all good things it has its downside, as Samantha's story illustrates.

It is shocking to think that 210,000 people are reported to the police in Britain as missing each year. This year The Missing Person Network are actively persuing 1,800 cases. Last week they launched a 'Get Together' campaign to enlist the help of cyperspacers to try to trace some of those gone AWOL.

Every year, there are in excess of 5,000 people reported missing in Ireland to the Gardaí. The majority of these cases are resolved. For the sixty to seventy cases that are not resolved, their families must live with uncertainty, with the pain of absence, with the hoping against hope that the lost one will return. When someone you love disappears without explanation, a nightmare journey, without a known destination, begins. Death is always a sad event but it can be ritualised. It is surrounded with the comforting support of family and friends. Just disappearing is different! When a relative goes missing, he or she takes with them a precious piece of those they have left behind. The umbilical cord with one's origins, history, traditions and place is severed. Everyone in the missing persons scenario is damaged. Of course, anyone over eighteen, who is in full health with a good mental capacity, is entitled to go missing. Apart from the missing – those who step into a black hole – there is a huge number of people who for one reason or another simply 'disconnect' from relatives and friends and place.

I was idly surfing the web some months ago when I came across the site www.missing.ws. It made for very sad reading. I tried to put myself in the place of the relatives left behind; to experience the anguish they were feeling. Fr Aquinas Duffy of the Dublin Diocese set up this website 'to help find his cousin Aengus Shanahan who was missing, and also to provide the facility for other Irish people to place their information'. He writes: 'the word "missing" in no way describes the sense of helplessness, frustration, anger and despair that goes through one's mind. Always, there is the desire to know where he or she is now and what happened to him or her. If one is a person of faith, then it is a real challenge to one's faith. It makes one realise that we depend on each other and that's why we need your help and ask you to keep your eyes open and on the look out for those who are missing. If you are a person who is missing, please do phone home or contact this webmaster. It is enough to know that you are alive and your privacy will be respected.'

Please visit this website. If there is someone missing in your area, has effective use been made of parish newsletters to publicise the missing person and to advertise the website? The pain doesn't go away. Those who remain need your support.

Mobile Phones – A Twenty-First Century Plague

The mobile phone is an irritant to many and contributes to bad manners.

'We are happy today to welcome this child into the Christian …' The tones of 'Waltzing Matilda' fill the chapel. The godfather has left his mobile phone on. He smirks with embarrassment as he fumbles in each pocket in turn. His mates in the congregation laugh uproariously. 'Waltzing Matilda' plays on.

Another scenario. 'Oh, sorry, would you mind just holding on a sec? I've just got to take this call on my mobile. Hello? Hello? Yes, yes, speaking. Oh hi … yes, dinner would be lovely. Thursday? That's fine. Who else is coming? Oh great! I would love to meet him. I've got to dash – I have someone with me. Bye, bye, bye bye. Sorry about that,' is the sheepish excuse to the irritated customer.

Rudeness, discourtesy, even unkindness go hand-in-hand with the mobile phone. The mobile phone is the greatest wrecker of traditional courtesies ever invented. Having a nice browse in a bookshop is no longer the pleasure it once was. Walking in a park, strolling on a beach, praying in a church –

nowhere is sacred from the creeping plague of the mobile phone. It is the Black Death of modern society. Why should I have to hear about Martha's success in her Leaving, Brian's new golf swing, the wonderful party Jane threw for her friends last night or John's prepared stance in a court case he is travelling to? I can recall reading in an article in *The Sunday Times* that only one-quarter of us write thank-you notes, half of us are habitually late, and 46 per cent of us screen other party guests before accepting an invitation. Why have we become so rude? The coarsening of Ireland has largely eliminated respect.

Why is it that we don't mind using our mobile phone at the table in a restaurant? This, by anyone's standards, is inconsiderate to fellow diners. The sad fact is that we have very little spontaneous and natural reaction for the feelings of others. Sitting in a golf club that displayed a prominent sign 'No Mobile Phones' didn't deter a priest friend taking two calls within earshot of members and visitors in a crowded room. 'Par for the course' might be an appropriate comment! It was plainly obvious that the impropriety of what he was doing simply didn't register. Despite the fact that mobiles are equipped with voice mail, the scourge of the instant compels us to answer every call immediately.

Celtic Tiger Ireland in which one's worth is measured by one's possessions, the value of one's house and the glossiness of one's children has also spurred on selfish individualism: people no longer regard reticence, humility and moderation as virtues. 'If you have it, flaunt it' is the mantra of our newly liberated society. Bah! Humbug! All social intercourse is coarsened by competitiveness rather than being lubricated by consideration of how the other person might feel. Looking after Number One has swept aside traditional courtesies. Everyone is on first-name terms with everyone else, even at a first meeting. Ever queue for a DART at peak time? The scramble for places would do justice to an Irish front-row scrum in a Grand Slam final. The weak are scattered in the frenzied rush for the doors. There is very little room left for kindness or courtesy.

I hate the 'when I was your age' waffle that we older people frequently engage in. Nevertheless an abiding memory of mine is the annual reading in the seminary refectory of a little tome entitled 'Courtesy for Clerics'. We were shown how to hold a knife and fork, how to lay a table, modes of address and the many ways of displaying kindness and consideration for others. Where are people taught basic manners today? In the home?

Modern psychobabble, which encourages us all to boost our self-esteem, has the unfortunate effect of encouraging the egoists in our midst to display even less consideration for others and even more absorption in themselves. Dare I say that I have serious reservation in regard to much of the 'assertiveness' training courses peddled these days. I have seen the soft, courteous side of people's personality being transformed into a bullying type of attitude that is determined to come out on top come what may.

An American proverb says that 'the test of good manners is being able to put up with bad ones'. The use or abuse of the mobile should be set into the wider scenario of good manners generally. In my young days good manners were fitted into the context of the indwelling of Jesus in each person. Mother Teresa called the poor 'Jesus in his distressing disguise'. Being mannerly

MARTIN TIERNEY

recognises the dignity of the other. One of the most motivating sayings in scripture must be 'as long as you did it to one of these the least of my brethren you did it to me'. Perhaps the rudeness in the use of mobile phone is just an indication of a wider malaise?

Moving Statues

*Of all the strange phenomena in twentieth-century
Ireland, that of the 'moving statues' is stranger than
fiction.*

At the end of July 1985 I got a phone call from Long Island,
New York. At the other end of the phone a lazy America drawl
called out, 'What about those moving statues then?' I asked who
was calling. 'My name is Doug Palmer,' came the reply. 'I am a
movie script writer and would like to do something on the
moving statues.' Only after a number of telephone calls and a
face-to-face meeting with Doug did I persuade him that this
phenomenon was in all probability a passing one. I suggested
that he would be well advised to keep his talents, money and
initiative for other projects.

Seven people, out for an evening stroll, stopped at the grotto in
the parish of Ballinspittle in south-west Cork, to recite a decade
of the rosary. The statue of Our Lady moved! This was the
catalyst that convulsed the country in an orgy of statue chasing
that left some laity and many clerics perplexed. Ballinspittle
became the epicenter of a 'gabfest' in which the entire country

participated. People came in their thousands, some with binoculars, others with stools for a long wait or black plastic bags to protect themselves from the chilly dank soil of the nearby hillside. Few doubted that they saw an erratic motion of the head and shoulders of the statue. Here before their very eyes a half a ton of concrete was moving without the involvement of any outside agent. Psychlogists from UCC came to observe and said that 'the statue only appeared to move'. It was an optical illusion. Others said it was 'auto-suggestion'. Some claimed that the whole phenomenon was damaging to the faith. Theologians were mystified – here were people coming to worship at a 'moving statue', while at the same time many of them remained away from Mass, the greatest of all mysteries.

A letter to *The Irish Times* read, 'How can the young see their elders, who are supposedly practising Catholics, behaving as if they were primitive tribes people mesmerised by the druids?' T.P. O'Mahony, then religious correspondent of the *Irish Press*, wrote, 'My own view is that it's quite a disturbing phenomenon. It really would make you wonder what people are at – I would say the whole exercise is bordering on the superstitious'. Peter Prendergast, the Government's then press secretary, commented cynically, 'Three-quarters of the country is laughing heartily' at the antics of those folk in the south and west. The rustics, according to the Dublin enlightenment, had got it wrong again!

It is only when history comes to be written that a true appreciation of the effects of the frenetic change of the past few decades will be appreciated. We came from a monolithic, church-based, confident, albeit deprived, society. We were certain about our beliefs. In the 1970s and 1980s all that we took as certain was being challenged. Have you ever had an arm amputated? We all know the depth of despair on the death of one we love. Here we were being robbed of the spirit before our eyes. We were being amputated from what we considered to be an essential part of who we were. The theft of spiritual meaning destroys us at every level – the individual, the family, the neighbourhood, the culture, the nation, the fate of the world. The theft of the spirit disables us physically and emotionally. We wanted to believe and we sought a sign. We needed the reassurance that Ballinspittle seemed to provide. A massive confrontation between the forces of the enlightenment, or Dublin 4, as the rustics would have it, and the old order of Church, republicanism and the GAA was happening. Some would say the 'soul of Ireland' was at stake. Moving statues was the last throw of the dice by the Hibernian remnant. I don't believe anything happened at Ballinspittle. However, I appreciate and understand why the phenomenon happened and how it was a sign of consolation and hope to many people. Ballinspittle was manna to a desperation experienced but not expressed.

It is through ritual that we separate our ordinary selves from our extraordinary possibilities. We create the sacred time necessary to address important questions with the attention they deserve. All around us people, family members, were abandoning rituals and practices hallowed by centuries of tradition. Ballinspittle was a reassurance that it was all right to hold on to the piety of a past most were abandoning.

THE MYTH OF SELF-ESTEEM

*Undoubtedly good self-esteem is important, but could
it be possible that we attribute too much of our ills to
low self-esteem?*

When I was young 'self-esteem' was not part of the English
lexicon. Sure, I felt pretty bad when I failed examinations, didn't
make the football team or thought my talents weren't being
recognised. However, I cannot remember a time when I
imagined that a negative self-image was holding me back in life.
I just tried harder in the areas where I had some chance of
success. Nowadays, there are no bad people but only people who
think badly of themselves. The shelves of our bookstores are
chock-a-block with books to help you feel better about yourself.
The mantra is that, 'If you really accept yourself nothing can
make you unhappy'. The experts tell us that deviant behaviour
can easily be explained away by poor self-image. Over-
indulgence in alcohol, promiscuous behaviour and greed are not
bad things, but rather *prima facie* evidence of self-image
problems. Many churches have discovered that 'low self-esteem'
is less off-putting than 'sin'. Is it any wonder that there is no sin

anymore? People are now seeing so many things – teenage pregnancies, youth homelessness and drug abuse – as evidence of low self-esteem. Even big corporations have latched on to the self-esteem syndrome.

This self-esteem syndrome is allied to the positive thought school of philosophy. Positive thinking, they say, can right wrongs even in ten-year-old girls and boys. Undoubtedly self-esteem is very important. Without a positive view of one's own capabilities and talents life could become frustratingly sterile. Norman Vincent Peale gave self-esteem (or positive thinking) a religious dimension. This was picked up by Robert Schuller of the Crystal Cathedral, who said that 'people who do not love themselves can't believe in God'. Some Christians caught up in the positive thinking school of living say that 'the great sin is not the things that people typically see as sins, it's not living up to their own potential'. Leaders in business say that 'self esteem is a basic building block on which personal effectiveness is based'.

In my day I attended a lot of courses built on the positive thinking/self-esteem or therapy for the ego. At the time I was excited by the possibilities offered by many of the quasi-New Age philosophies. Is it possible to power one's self on a daily basis with a shot of 'self-esteem', much like a diabetic taking their insulin? The human person naturally experiences valleys and troughs in daily living. There are happenings that cause pain and upset, as well as others that give pleasure, peace and happiness. To substitute a real relationship for the 'how to win friends and influence people' philosophy is a shallow stance towards life. Something more is needed. American gurus like Jess Lair with a Ph.D. after their name pump out books like,

I ain't much, baby – but I'm all I've got, which promises us that we can turn the corner into a more beautiful life – five minutes at a time. Would that it were that easy. The book of Sirach says, 'When you come to serve the Lord prepare yourselves for trials' – a different message from a different author.

In Ireland, the Catholic Church could be excused if it had 'self-image' problems. We are assaulted on a daily basis by a rather hostile media, arguably unprecedented in the Western world.

Nevertheless there are few stories that don't contain an element of truth. Blaming the messenger rather than discerning the message is a sterile activity. Developing a persecution complex may be a guaranteed way of developing a poor self-image as a church.

Our self-esteem is built not on the chimera of public opinion or perception, but on a belief in the fidelity of God's love for us. Everyone is a VIP in the eyes of God. We need good public relations, but even more we need a deep belief that 'for those who love God all things work together unto good'.

THE NEED FOR FRIENDSHIP

Friendship is a place where the core issues of life can be shared.

The colour supplement of an English newspaper recently published a feature on people who live in hotels. For these people the hotel is home. The hotel provides all the facilities they need – food, laundry, cleaning and telephone. Some are the super-rich, for whom a suite in Claridge's or a penthouse apartment in the Ritz in Paris is nothing unusual. Others are poor asylum seekers who live in dilapidated run-down hovels that hardly merit the name 'hotel'. Then there are those who simply can't cope with living alone – sometimes they are single or their life partner has died. Hotel living, they feel, is their only option. They all have one thing in common: they are friendless. Their impoverished and isolated living is troubling and sad. It is not good for man or woman to be alone; something more is needed.

The growth of chat rooms on the internet says something about the loneliness of life for many people. Locked in a room, gazing transfixed at a computer monitor for hours is a sorry substitute for real friends. And yet for millions worldwide the internet is their surrogate friend. They browse, night after night, for the consolation of human contact. There are those who are fearful of the risk of being a friend of anyone and thereby suffer a deprivation of spirit.

Is friendlessness one of the plagues of the twenty-first century? Is it the plague that dare not speak its name? The anonymity of apartment living in a big city is tailor-made for isolation and friendlessness. Some people are described as 'loners'. I often wonder if being a loner is a deliberately chosen stance towards life or simply an inability to reach out and embrace the friendship of others. I hear endless talk of not intruding on 'a person's space'. Such talk leaves many of us fearful of establishing the contact that could be the kiss of life. Friendship is the outer movement towards involvement and participation. Friendship is a joy, but it is also a responsibility.

The word 'friend' is so much deeper and richer than the word 'acquaintance' or even 'love'. Acquaintances are little more than ships passing in the night. We have many acquaintances but few friends. Friendship is a matter of the heart where our innermost thoughts, fears, anxieties and joys dwell. Because friendship is a thing of the heart, of a sacred place, it has a fearful dimension to it. Friendship is a place where the core issues of life can be shared. This is fearful because a matter of the heart once shared can never be recalled. At the heart of friendship is trust. It is saying to the other person, I trust you with this part of me. It is a vote of confidence. A friend is someone you can ring up at 4 a.m. in the morning! Nowadays we hear a lot about intimacy, almost as if it were something that could be programmed or achieved according to a predetermined systematic formula. *Men are from Mars, Women are from Venus*, a very popular book some years ago, claimed to lay such ground rules for growth in friendship. But friendship has its own organic growth: it is a pilgrim journey with rewards unimagined. It nurtures, supports, nourishes and corrects.

There is an ache in the human heart for friendship. The world is lonely. The website Friends Reunited has nine times more participants than the Church of England in any given week – 15 per cent of the UK is registered! Lebanese poet Kahlil Gibran writes of friendship, 'all thoughts, all desires, all expectations are born and shared, with joy that is unacclaimed'. The great Indian writer Tagore wrote of friendship like this: 'You have made me known to friends whom I knew not. You have given me seats in homes not my own. You have brought the distant near and made a brother of the stranger.' Jesus has given us an example of the possibilities contained within the mystery of true friendship. One of the most poignant scenes in the Gospel is the sobbing of Jesus at the death of his friend Lazarus. His tears would never have flowed unless both had risked the letting go that true friendship demands.

THE NEW AGE

Shirley MacLaine started a real 'fad' that has attracted millions when she spawned the movement called the 'New Age'.

They flocked to the RDS in their thousands. The recent Mind, Body, Spirit Fair was like a magnet to a new generation of 'searchers'. They came to the Mecca of Irish show jumping in Ballsbridge, not for horses, but seeking self-fulfilment. With the decline of conventional religion in many parts of the Western world, an affluent generation, mainly women, has gone on a spending spree to give meaning to their lives. Not all, but some are Chanel-clad, clasping personal organisers, who want the spiritual goods, want them quickly and are prepared to pay the price. One in five British women between the ages of thirty-five and forty-four regularly turn to prayer – but not Christian prayer, as we have traditionally known it. Judging by the numbers at the RDS, women here are running strongly to catch up with their UK sisters. Perhaps a generation ago women would be at home with three or four children and wouldn't have had time to worry about why life wasn't too fulfilling. I may be wrong, but I feel that the insecurities and uncertainties that we all struggle with may be exploited by a new brand of entrepreneurs who have found a niche market that reaps rich rewards. Women and men now in executive positions, with considerable spending power, are looking to fill a hole in their lives. For many of them there is always just one more healer or psychic or spiritual counsellor to try. Their growing quest for spiritual solace fuels a consumer boom that delights the entrepreneurs. Tony Quinn, the doyen of Ireland's New Age gurus, started out as a yoga instructor, a position invested with an aura of divinity, and now has an empire of 'health food shops' dotted in the most fashionable shopping malls in the country.

Along with their clothes, entertainment and household expenses, many women are now adding a spiritual budget that can run into several hundreds of euro a week. Cherie Blair had one, Princess Diana had one – a personal spiritual New Age guru to help them along the way. At the more modest end of the market, a crystal healing session can cost as little as €45. A Reiki session, to realign the body's energy, relieve pain and promote spiritual clarity, can cost as little as €34 a session. Aromatherapy, now mainstream, uses oils to restore lost balance to mind, body and soul. Most Catholic retreat houses in Ireland have a variety of New Age programmes on offer in their brochures.

While individual spiritual treatments are rarely more expensive than a trip to the hairdresser, the bills start to add up for a complete spiritual fix. There is a limit to the treatment that hair can take; by contrast, the spirit can absorb everything you can afford to throw at it.

A range of alternative treatments and a coterie of mystics can help alleviate stress. Feeling jaded? Hold a crystal in your hands

MARTIN TIERNEY

and give your energy a boost. Need someone to talk to? Phone your healer. Unsure about your decision? Phone your astrologer. Why not try iridology? It is based on a belief that a corresponding area in the iris of the eye represents each area of the body. Practitioners study the pigment flecks to diagnose ailments. Some of the practitioners of New Age therapies manage to maintain a link, however tenuous, with their Catholic past. Some of the new therapies are designed around the release of 'cosmic energy'. For 'cosmic energy', in some cases, substitute 'God' – the terms can be interchangeable.

Many of the people who frequent New Age gatherings are spiritually sensitive people. They are open to the transcendent. There is a hunger in their lives for the spiritual dimension of living. They are drawn to the hocus pocus of New Age because they can see little else to fill the spiritual void in their lives. The fact that there is seldom an official Church presence at rock festivals or New Age gatherings may indicate that it is not the New Agers who have abandoned the Church, but we who have abandoned them. It is easy for church-goers to judge the New Age as 'appealing but illusory'. More than criticism is needed. New Age people feel not just let down by the Church but by traditional medicine. No longer are they prepared to be the 'heart case in bed 13,' or told to 'pop a pill' daily; they are looking for something more personal in their treatment.

There is a world of difference between what happened last weekend in the RDS and what happened in the Roman Catholic Churches in the surrounding district. Within the plethora of New Age therapies there is the possibility for men and women to minister to people in need. They feel they are providing solace;

whether this is illusory or not, is not the point. They are helpers by nature. Their instincts are ones of service. In the church on Sunday, apart from reading or distributing the Eucharist, there is very little scope for direct one-to-one ministry for lay people. The ministries within our Church are based on function or office rather than charism. Are the gifts of the Holy Spirit only given to the ordained? Can a lay person get the gift of healing? Can a lay person receive the gift of preaching and teaching? Is there room enough in our Church for the exercise of spiritual ministry by lay people?

THE POPE'S VISIT

The whole of Ireland was caught up in a frenzy of delight in September 1979 when the Pope came to visit.

The Greek philosopher Heraclitus wrote, 'you cannot step into the same river twice'. What happened in Ireland on the last week of September 1979 was a once-off event of stupendous magnitude, the like of which is possibly unrepeatable. *The Irish Times* headlined the reaction of the people as 'outpourings of joy and fervour'. The changing times since that historic visit is best characterised by an editorial in the *Irish Independent*: 'a feeling of great loneliness swept through the land yesterday when the doors of the aircraft carrying Pope John Paul closed, as the plane taxied and as it took off, bringing with it a man we will never see again on this island.' This wasn't a fanciful caricature of the prevailing mood. It accurately summarised the bond we all felt had been forged between Pope John Paul and ourselves during those exhilarating autumn days.

Nobody wanted to be left out. Offers of help, most of them offered gratuitously, piled in as the event drew nearer. As a member of the Dublin committee, I get a warm feeling inside as I reflect on the depth of the generosity of countless people. The late Bishop Carroll, our chairman, ever a gentleman, was meticulous in his attention to detail. Public officials were unfailingly helpful. In a time before greed gripped the Irish heart there was a willingness to give without counting the cost. Business people wanted to make a contribution and many of them did, mostly anonymously. Groups like the Irish Management Institute and the Public Relations Institute of Ireland made their expertise available. Government departments like Defence and Post and Telegraphs made sure that our country would perform at the highest level of professionalism. In was a nightmare for the Gardaí. Security arrangements were the tightest ever experienced south of the border. I know of one exasperated cleric who leaked to the media in order to try to move the security logjam. Meeting after meeting was attended in a spirit of joyful resignation. In the parishes the preparation was done with a thoroughness we shouldn't forget. I can still recall hearing confessions in the Vincentian Church in Phibsborough on the night before the Pope's arrival and being overwhelmed by the humility of the people. Many of them were returning to the sacrament after a considerable time. The noise of footsteps padding towards the Park in the dark of an autumn morning is what most of us remember.

What effect did the Pope's visit leave? Very little. The notice of the visit was very short. Everyone's energies were focused on the immediate preparations for what was to happen in September. It was nobody's fault that depleted energies simply couldn't rise to an effective spiritual follow-up. The best and the

MARTIN TIERNEY

brightest had given everything. The visit was a resounding success but it left little or no legacy. Much of the Pope's prophetic teaching went unheeded. Having said that, I believe that there are hidden testimonies of conversions and graces from that visit that remain to be heard.

Two personal vignettes come to mind. At that time I was a member of the Irish Aero Club and colleagues, like thousands of others, offered their services. The Club was asked to fly the vestments from the Mass in the Park to Ballybrit for the youth Mass in Galway. Getting down was easy compared to the return journey. After the Mass every inch of road space was clogged with heaving humanity. Our car to the airfield for the return journey remained stationary for at least two hours. The weather was deteriorating; the vestments had to return to Dublin for the Maynooth event on the following day. Exasperation turned to hopelessness until one bright wit thought of an idea. 'Why not commandeer an ambulance,' he asked innocently. It was done. An understanding ambulance crew helped us load the vehicle with the vestment boxes, we all crammed in behind and, with siren blaring, we edged our way to the airfield. The weather looked ominous. A fine mist from a blanket of murky grey clouds made flying visually hazardous. We took off in five Cessna aircraft and found our way to Dublin by flying too low for comfort over the Galway to Dublin railway line. Biggles and his sidekick Ginger would have been proud of us!

Another of my memories of the Papal Mass in the Phoenix Park was the grand larceny of the specially made pottery ciboria used for distributing Holy Communion. It was a case of 'now you see them, now you don't'! As the Pope drove around the corrals to the delight of the people, clerics were furtively concealing ciboria under their clerical garb and making a dash for it! As well as the obligatory photo of 'me and the Pope' hanging on the wall by the fireside, many presbyteries now proudly display a ciborium from the Park, stolen unfortunately. Restitution is still awaited!

Religious Symbols have Lost their Meaning

Unlike the global brands we encounter every day, church symbolism fails to connect with the twenty-first-century Catholic.

At the height of the depression in 1937, the McDonald brothers opened a small cinema, but it quickly went bust. As far as they could tell the only business making money at the time was a nearby hot-dog stand run by a man named Walker Wiley. So they opened a stand near the Santa Anita racetrack. They did well from the start. McDonalds are now on course to turn the Big Mac into a global brand to rival Coke. In February 1999 Georgia became the one hundred and fifteenth country to play host to those trademark golden arches. The golden arches have become a symbol for quick service, cleanliness and quality 'junk' food. The symbol is recognised everywhere.

The holiday that changed the face of international highways occurred in the summer of 1951. Kemmons Wilson took his family on vacation. They had real difficulty finding suitable places to stay. Day by day on the trip, Wilson became more irritated, until he finally turned to his wife Dorothy and announced he was going into the hotel business. He saw Bing Crosby's Holiday Inn on television and that was the beginning. At one point he was building a new Holiday Inn every two and a half days. The Holiday Inn symbol with its distinctive script is recognised for cheap, no-frills holiday accommodation worldwide.

Symbols and chants contain meaning: 'You'll never walk alone' from the Kop at the Liverpool football ground is recognisable to fans world-wide; 'Rule Britannia' brims with post-colonial jingoism, conjuring up images of retired majors home from the Second Afghan War or the Punjab, sipping sundowners on their verandas in the Shires. When an athlete makes the sign of the cross before a big race, I am certain that millions of people worldwide, Catholic or not, know that this is religious symbolism. The cross is a universal symbol of Christ and Christianity.

But the religious symbols used in liturgical celebrations today are not widely understood. The tiny wafer and drop of wine used at Mass don't speak to that many people, neither do vestments or rituals that are so specifically religious that many non-churchgoers simply do not understand them. I was speaking to a sociologist recently who had just completed a survey of 17 to 25 year olds on faith and culture. He told me that 'young people have lost the language and vocabulary of faith'. The symbols and the language of liturgy are incomprehensible to a growing number of people. Nevertheless, where these symbols retain their meaning the devotion is obvious.

The Eucharist is referred to as sacrament, as a sacrifice or as a sacred meal. I'm pretty sure what is meant in each case, but what about those who still attend church or indeed those who don't? The new liturgy regards the bread and wine not just as objects

Martin Tierney

but gifts, 'what earth has given and human hands have made'. They are brought to our altar 'as signs of our existence, for through them we wish to place in the hands of our Maker our entire existence'. How many people in our churches next Sunday know this? If there is no offertory procession or if it is done in a careless and sloppy manner, how can it speak to the people? I do not think that religious symbols have to be secularised – they have to be explained.

In recent years the sales of candles have burgeoned. A candle has become an indispensable symbol of intimacy, of calmness, of peace. I know people who come home from work exhausted. They light candles around the home, place an aromatic perfume in the oil burner, put on some soothing music and just relax. This is their way of recovering from a busy day. These symbols have meaning. They speak of peace and tranquility. Thankfully the lighting of candles has remained a powerful prayer symbol in the Church.

Many religions use incense. I can recall being absolutely amazed in Singapore at the number of business men and women who thronged the Buddhist Temple, lit a stick of incense and paused for a moment of silence before hurrying to work. Incense has all but disappeared from our churches, though I do believe it still retains its potency as a powerful symbol of prayer and worship.

The Grand Synagogue in Jerusalem has the most elaborate ceremonials surrounding the scrolls of the Torah. They look on these massive scrolls with awe and reverence. There is real drama here! A non-Jewish onlooker is only waiting for what is to come next. Certainly, for me, the sacredness of the word, for the Jewish worshipper, could not be mistaken.

Symbols do not have to be elaborate. I know when one is beginning the Tohar Padraig from Ballintubber to Croagh Patrick one is advised to take a small stone before leaving the Abbey. This stone represents the hopes and desires of the pilgrim. Arriving at the sacred mountain the stones are left in a neat pile as an offering, symbolic of one's openness to change and one's intention for the pilgrimage. Then the pilgrim takes another small stone to take home. This represents an area of one's life that needs to be handed over to the Lord. It remains a constant reminder of a promise given to God.

Thankfully there are some wonderfully creative people in our Church who have been working tirelessly to promote the use of symbolism in worship. We even had a new-born lamb in a crib in a local church on Good Shepherd Sunday recently!

Robbing Parents of their Rights

There are worrying indications that the state is encroaching on what were formerly the rights of parents. More and more young people are targeted by marketing, big business and the state, thereby potentially corroding the rights of parents.

Today in the West we're being engaged in an experiment that's never been tried before; a world where marriage is optional, stable families increasingly rare and almost all the responsibilities of parenthood can be delegated away: education to schools, law enforcement to police, care to childminders or welfare agencies and recreation to TV and radio. It is time to shout 'Stop!' I am convinced that we are not delegating parental responsibilities to others; they are in fact being stolen from us. The subtle erosion of parental rights and responsibilities by state agencies leads to a 'nanny state', which becomes mother and father to the child. For instance, there is seldom any discussion on whose right it is to give sex education. I would have thought that the right is fundamentally that of the parents. Where did the state get the authority to usurp that which belongs rightly to parents? It is understandable that some parents allow this right to be taken from them because it is an area where so many feel inadequate. But what about those parents who wish to exercise their right to educate their children in this area? Are they to be summarily dismissed as 'fuddy duddies'? It is not just in the area of sex education that the rights of parents are being undermined. Last year a student went to the local school to collect his Leaving Cert results. At the school gates a local hostelry was distributing handouts advertising free drinks for students to celebrate their results. It is really difficult for good parents to protect their sons and daughters from the crass greed of those who willingly exploit them.

In America the average child spends approximately four hours a day watching television and only forty minutes a week talking to their parents. I am not sure if the situation is any different here. In the words of Robert Reich, Professor of Public Policy at the University of California, the family, like the business corporation, is being downsized and outsourced. Rarely has parenthood been surrounded by so much confusion. It is slipping in public esteem, and this should not happen. It's bad news. I admire those parental organisations that refuse to allow government agencies or others to usurp their authority and are willing to take a stand in an area of supreme importance.

It was the Bible that gave the world the idea that God isn't just a power but also a parent. We call him our Father. As God said through the prophet Isaiah, 'like one whom his mother comforts, so will I comfort you'. I loved the comment of one mother who said to me recently, 'Since I've become a parent I can relate more closely to God. Now I know what it's like to create something you can't control'. In the one verse in the Bible that explains why God chose Abraham to be the founder of a new faith, it says, 'I have chosen him so that he will teach his children and his household after him to keep the ways of the Lord, doing what is right and just'. What made Abraham and Sarah special in God's eyes was simply that they understood the responsibilities of parenthood. God is both father and mother, the one to whom many parents look for inspiration and guidance.

Without good parenting, even the best school and the finest teachers may fail. Even the most talented young person faces emotional crises in life. Giving time to children outweighs in value the goods of this world that are usually lavished upon them. The biggest bouncy castle for the birthday party, the most gorgeous dress for the First Communion, the latest Play Station and the newest Nike runners are the compensations given to children for lapsed parenting. There is no more awesome responsibility than bringing new life into the world and, having done so, we can't just walk away and leave the rest to others. The ground already given away has got to be regained. It will demand that parents challenge the political correctness of the day and make their voices heard. Shakespeare had it right when he wrote, 'The voice of parents is the voice of gods, for to their children they are heaven's lieutenants …'.

THE SALVATION ARMY

The Salvation Army found a new way of sharing the gospel at the most unlikely of places – the Chelsea Flower Show.

The Chelsea Flower Show is the mother of all shows. This Olympics for the green fingered annually attracts a worldwide crowd. Hosted by the Royal Horticultural Society, this annual 'sell out' features kitchen gardens, flower beds, indoor plants, shrubs, lawns, pond gardens and spectacular sponsored designer gardens costing a small fortune. Some years ago there was something different. The Salvation Army was rewarded with a Silver Medal picked up at the Show for a garden entitled 'from Darkness to Light'. The six deep crowds thronging around it throughout the show made it one of the exhibits impossible to get a close look at without some unChristian elbowing and foot treading of rival viewers. What a wonderfully creative bit of evangelising by the Salvation Army! When it comes to sowing the seeds of faith the Salvation Army has always been one of the most innovative Christian groups around.

The Sally Army was present at the Show with a brass band, which for the occasion included celebrities like James Galway.

It used the annuals and perennials to illustrate the universal religious themes of transience and eternity. The garden was designed to express their Christian faith that Christ came to draw us from darkness into light. The substantial sponsorship needed for the garden was raised from a British firm Buildbase. I was intrigued by this tit-bit of topical news because I am in the middle of reading, *Blood and Fire*, the biography of William and Catherine Booth, the founders of the Salvation Army. Former Labour politician Roy Hattersley authors this most readable book. Hattersley is the son of a Roman Catholic priest and professes himself an unbeliever.

William Booth's success was built on a single-minded certainty: all that mattered was saving souls. Even when he began to take a concern for the underprivileged he viewed this as a way of smoothing their path to heaven. Booth, and his wife Catherine, ministered in the middle of the nineteenth century at a time when British colonial expansion was at its zenith. This was the Empire on which 'the sun never set'. It was a time when young missionaries spent their lives acquiring, building up, supplying and teaching in schools of every description. Hospitals were built and staffed by nuns. Following the Raj reaped fertile conversions to the Catholic Church. After all, there was a thirst for learning and people needed healing. Some would claim that there was an element of 'souperism' in some of this missionary endeavour.

Now that schools and hospitals are out of the hands of religious, at home and effectively worldwide, how is the Church to proclaim the Gospel? I have heard calls for evangelisation, yet we still send the best and brightest to study Canon Law! Serious and significant efforts at primary evangelisation have been made in Europe, particularly in France, yet I am still waiting to hear of anyone, religious or lay person, being sent to study missionary methods on the continent of Europe. In France a flourishing community, Emmanuel, began on a barge in the Seine in the late 1960s. Apart from a flourishing and life-giving liturgy it has produced many vocations to the priesthood for the diocese of Paris. It has a ministry to families that in a thoroughly secularised society must be a jewel in the crown of the Church in Europe. Has anyone been sent to study what is happening there? William Booth took the unprecedented step of preaching in pubs and clubs. He went where he was confident he could gather a crowd. He was a man of new ideas and exciting experiments.

There are seasoned schools of evangelisation in Europe. The best-known of which is the International School of Catholic Evangelisation, approved by the Vatican, and based in Malta and Germany. Some Irish lay people have graduated from these schools but their expertise has not been utilised or officially supported in the Irish context. Why not? Youth with a Mission has just completed a Discipleship Training School in Dublin and the young men and women attending the school were admirable in their missionary efforts. I could not fail to pay tribute to difficult work of Catholic Youth Care in Dublin.

It was William Booth who pioneered the strategy of using the poor to recruit the poor – reformed sinners who brought the unredeemed salvation, what we call like-to-like ministry. He found that men who would never consider entering a church were prepared to listen to a rousing sermon if it was delivered from the stage of a derelict music hall or the tap-room of what had once been a public house. He recruited reformed drunks, redeemed prostitutes and discharged felons to give testimony about how they had benefited from acquiring virtue. The Salvation Army idea of a missionary movement with military pretensions was one adopted by Frank Duff for the Legion of Mary. Uniforms, bands and banners made the Salvation Army irresistible to the more romantic Victorian poor. He brightened the gloomiest corner of England, the East End of London, where he laboured with brightness and the gaiety of God. We have a lot to learn from evangelical Christian groups who have been pioneering a ministry of evangelisation for many years.

Say it with Flowers

Flowers remind us of beautiful moments in life.
Gardening, like painting, brings life to the soul.

I was looking at some very old black-and-white photographs of the house and garden where I was brought up as a child. They weren't quite sepia but each had the yellowish tinge of age. I drew from my memory bank the shrieks of children having fun. Then I was struck by something peculiar – the absence of flowers. Yes, that was it! A few wispy plants, lonely and forlorn, were the garden's complement. Close by where our family lived was what was then called a 'market garden', run by the last remaining ascendancy family of the area. In summer the Hume-Dudgeons who owned this well-tended garden sold vegetables and soft fruits to surrounding families. All now lie beneath the modern complex of University College Dublin. I have absolutely no recollection of flowers, shrubs or plants being for sale. Flower Shows were the preserve of fruity-voiced High Anglican women in straw hats, who were generally members of the Royal Dublin Society.

I think we were impoverished by the absence of the riotous colour of flowers that bedeck so many of our gardens, towns and villages now. Today visiting a Garden Centre can be as hectic an experience as dropping into Clery's on the first week of a Winter Sale. Close by where I lived is a well-run drinking emporium. I was immediately impressed by the dramatic impact of the lovingly-tended window boxes. Flowers of every colour of the spectrum tumble from the windows. 'Come drink with us' is the subtle message of the display. The colour entices people to believe that in this tavern you can expect to find a home-from-home.

Our recent love affair with flowers taps into the kernel of the soul. In a new report, 'A Plant a Day Keeps the Doctor Away', experts recommend a twenty-minute daily exposure to plants to maintain health and well-being – a sort of recommended daily allowance of greenery. Just like your five pieces of fruit and vegetables, or vitamins and minerals, plants are good for you. One study cited by the report claims that a couple of hours in the garden each day can reduce coronary heart disease and other chronic illnesses. In older people gardening also keeps mental ability sharp. Having something green to look at in hospital speeds a patient's recovery.

It is claimed that the greener and more natural a student's view from home, the better they score on tests of concentration, impulse inhibition and delayed gratification, i.e. self-discipline, a lack of which apparently is a predictor of delinquency, drug abuse, poor school marks and teenage pregnancy. It can't be an accident that a prison like Wheatfield has a garden and glasshouses.

Flowers, like songs or tunes, remind us of beautiful moments in life. *Bougainvillea* brings to mind balmy holidays by the Mediterranean. The blaze of gorse on the Wicklow hills warms the heart, even of emigrants far from home. The cactus of the high desert around New Mexico, where I spent some time once, is a grubby, obscure and humble vegetable, yet from its nest of thorns is born once each year a splendid flower. It is unpluckable, yet lovely, sweet and desirable. I once stayed for three months in an institution run by male religious. What I missed was the presence of living greenery. The corridors were filled with the rough carbolic smell of maleness. Flowers were only for women, was the message! Thankfully this is now the exception.

The award-winning entry of the Salvation Army at this year's Chelsea Flower Show was just wonderful. They believe that there are many ways of speaking of the wonder and glory of God apart from the pulpit. I agree with them. Visit a Church, and if the grounds or the sacristy, or indeed the church itself is neglected, a visitor is forced to question how serious the congregation is about the message being preached.

The beauty of flowers speaks of the glory and creativity of God. After all, it is God's creative power that keeps even the simplest daisy in being. To gaze at a rose can be a truly spiritual experience. The well-tended and flower-filled grounds of a parish church send out a life-giving message.

Gardening has now become an obsession. Numerous television and radio programmes sprinkle advice to wannabe gardeners. The enthusiasm brought by amateur gardeners to Gerry Daly's programme on a Saturday on RTÉ is infectious. Why should the Church lag behind in an enthusiasm that is so close to nature and to life? Life is what God is about and what Jesus promised. I once told a spiritual director that I was finding it difficult to pray. His advice was, 'Go for a walk, look at the trees and plants, reflect, and that will be your prayer for today'. On reflection I think it was wise advice!

MARTIN TIERNEY

SECOND MARRIAGES

Marriage breakdown is a fact of life. Naturally many seek happiness in a second marriage, but second relationships are no guarantee of happiness.

Patricia and Denis are friends of mine. Both have been through the scarifying experience of a marriage break-up. They are still raw. Such an experience can be worse than a death. With death, the loss is ritualised. Relatives and friends are at hand to sooth the grief. The Church is at its best in its comforting funeral rites. The break-up of a marriage invariably bequeaths a legacy of bitterness. The pain nags for a long time afterwards. It is understandable, perhaps even inevitable, that isolated and suffering people look elsewhere for the love that has been snatched from them. Patricia and Denis, both now divorced, have just got married again, this time in a Registry Office. Second time around holds out some hope for them. They are not aware that marriage is no easier second time around. I hadn't the heart to tell them. 'If your marriage is a second marriage, post-divorce, your second marriage is likelier to end in divorce' (Bronson and Merryman).

The incidence of marriage break-up in Britain has shifted from first to second marriages. To go through marriage break-up once is deeply traumatic; a second experience can strip the soul of hope. Yet that is what is happening. When Britain sneezes we catch the cold some years later. Marriage in Ireland may be looking into a bleak future if the trends of our nearest neighbour are replicated here. Figures released by the Office for National Statistics show that the number of divorces granted to couples where at least one party had been married before rose from 18,000 in 1981 to 27,595 in 2000. Among couples in which both partners had previously been divorced, the numbers getting a second divorce doubled in the same time. Statistically, Patricia and Denis are more likely to separate in this, their second chance, than they were first time around. Second marriages are almost twice as likely to break down as first marriages, third marriages almost three times as likely and fourth marriages almost four times as likely to fail. When it comes to marriage, practice does not make perfect.

Being separated can be an isolated, lonely place. It can be grim going to bed alone, without the comforting presence of a loving wife or husband. The consternation of coping single-handed with children and house can breed a longing for the support of a loving partner. After a divorce, people are very hurt and their self-esteem is flattened. They can feel a great sense of failure and they often look for somebody new to fill the great gap in their lives. Unfortunately many enter into a new relationship before they have resolved the problems that caused the break-up of their first marriage. This is all rational talk, whereas the emotional pain and the longing for love are gut feelings. The head seldom thinks clearly when the heart is aching.

MARTIN TIERNEY

Marriage break-up occurs in a welter of blame. To blame the former spouse for the failure of a marriage is par for the course. What many overlook is that the common denominator in all of this is themselves. They need to think hard about their role in the relationship breakdown before moving on. I am involved in a programme for people who are experiencing the pain of a marriage in trouble. Central to the programme is the attempt to generate a 'non-blaming' climate within which the couple can deal with the issues. There is only one person you can change in this life – yourself! Without some work on personal development it is more than likely that the fault lines of the first marriage will unwittingly be carried forward into the second relationship.

Couples who seek to end their misery by getting divorced are less likely to find lasting contentment than those prepared to work at their marriage. A recent piece of research by Linda Waite, a sociologist at the University of Chicago, suggests that the benefits of divorce have been hugely oversold. She writes, 'Our study found no evidence that unhappily married adults who divorced were typically any happier than unhappily married people who stayed married'. The data showed that those who stuck with their marriages were happier five years later than those who separated or divorced. This message needs to be sold.

I am seriously worried about the marriages of our young people. In the past eighteen months in a busy Dublin suburban parish, all, bar one, of the young couples that came to me for marriage papers had been living together for varying periods of time. I am unconvinced that cohabitation is a good preparation for marriage. Cohabitation can short-circuit the period of courtship, which can be a valuable exploratory period in any journey towards intimacy. Hormones ought not to be allowed to overrule reason.

The sacramental character of marriage ought to be a motivating factor for Christian couples to live a life of unselfish love. They are not alone. God's grace is with them. He desires their happiness. As long as we continue to compromise and shilly-shally about the essential requirements for a truly Christian marriage, present trends will continue and indeed worsen.

Sentenced to Meditation

A New Mexico judge sentenced an offender to a period
of meditation. Is meditation 'good for the soul'?

Santa Fe, the principal city of New Mexico, has a whimsical air about it. What makes the place unusual is that this city is the hub of worldwide New Age spirituality and an important centre for art and artists. It is also the capital of Native American culture. It is over ten years since I stayed there, and since then it has moved on in its quirky eccentricities. Recently, Santa Fe resident, Megan Rodriguez, pleaded guilty to a charge of domestic abuse in Santa Fe's Municipal Court. She had hurled a lamp at her live-in boyfriend. For this fairly mild misdemeanour she could expect a fine or the Probation Act in Ireland. Not in Santa Fe! Megan was sentenced to a Japanese tea ceremony, Thai chi classes, acupuncture and twelve weeks of meditation. Would you believe it? 'When I got the sentence, I kept thinking, what is the judge saying? Medi-what? A meditation sentence? I asked the court clerk if this was for real. I was sure I would get community service, cleaning litter or something,' said Megan. Psychologist Mark de Francis designed this novel form of punishment. Usual sentences such as imprisonment, community service or hefty fines simply weren't working. According to de Francis: 'Tai chi teaches them to slow down their physical bodies, the tea ceremony teaches them respect for and interaction with others. Meditation, through visualisation and breathing, shows them they can calm their minds. This is a new concept for them but very empowering.'

Yoga of all sorts is a technique growing massively in popularity throughout Ireland. It is becoming part of the curriculum in many schools, both Primary and Secondary. Parish halls countrywide now host a yoga class as part of their usual weekly activities. Indeed, New Age practices have seeped into mainstream thinking as techniques or coping mechanisms in this frenetic world. Is it any wonder that Santa Fe includes meditation as part of its sentencing policy? What has all this to say to the mainline Christian churches? People, religious or not, know that reflection ought to be part of every growing life. How is it that we have failed to persuade church-going people that silence, meditation, discernment and prayer is central to the Christian life?

There is a search for the transcendent. God has implanted eternity into the hearts of people. We long to know the Power beyond us and discover a reason for living beyond the boundaries of our mundane ordinariness. For many New Age groups this transcendence, or God, if you wish, is within. It is within in the sense that there is an identification of God with myself. I am God. All is God. When we hear expressions such as, 'Mother Earth crucified', beloved by former Dominican theologian Matthew Fox, we get an inkling of the pantheistic nature of much New Age thinking. According to this thinking, we are all one – God, the earth and ourselves. But this leaves no room for a Saviour. In fact, if we are all one, there is no need for a Saviour. There is no sin or virtue; no divisions; no boundaries. And so in New Age vocabulary 'God' is usually referred to as Cosmic Energy.

Recruiting meditation in the fight against crime might sound a typically wacky American fad. However, since the 1960s Western spirituality has been heavily influenced by Eastern religions. The Maharishi Mahesh Yogi, best known for introducing the Beatles to transcendental meditation, was indirectly an instrument in the foundation of the Natural Law Party who contested election both in Ireland and in Britain. Buddhism or Hinduism are behind many apparently mainstream establishments, such as the School of Philosophy and Economic Science, who advertise extensively in our Irish newspapers.

Our Church has an extraordinary mystical tradition and we have to find ways of opening this treasure house to the searching laity. The philosopher, writer and mystic, Simon Weil remarked, 'Society is a cave. The way out is solitude'. Some have learned to live in the monastery of the heart. New Age people have learned to live with solitude. Some have learned that one must go beyond words if one wishes to understand what lies behind the skin of things. They have also learned a restraint of the body in their fasting, diet and lifestyle. They left the Church behind, thinking that it had nothing to offer. The success of John Main's meditation technique is an indication that there is still a thirst for the transcendent within the Catholic tradition.

Embarking on the spiritual journey is like getting into a very small boat and setting out on the ocean to search for unknown lands. For all we know, when we get to the horizon, we are going to drop off the edge of the world. Like all explorers, we are drawn to discover what's waiting out there without knowing yet if we have the courage to face it. Because we preach a minimalist interpretation of the Gospel, the challenge to find out what the mystical tradition of Catholicism has to offer is rarely extended. We Catholics need the courage to launch out into the deep.

The Sante Fe Municipal Court got it right! We need to learn from the wisdom of that judge.

The Siberian Gulag

The story of Fr Walter Chiszek is one of faith, heroism and perseverance in the face of appalling suffering.

In the early 1970s I was in Long Island, New York. I was introduced to a man named Duffy (I cannot remember his Christian name). He kept talking about a priest named Fr Chiszek. He invited him to meet him. I was indifferent and didn't accept his invitation. This is now one of the regrets of my life. Thirty years later I was browsing on Amazon.com and out of nowhere the name Chiszek popped up! I immediately connected with Long Island all those years ago. The book being advertised was *He Leadeth Me* by Fr Walter Ciszek, published by Ignatius Press. I purchased it and read it in two days! This is a book I would make compulsory reading for every priest.

Captured in Poland by the Russian army during World War II, Chiszek, an American, was carted off to Moscow and incarcerated in the infamous Lubianka Prison. This prison, the responsibility of the hated NKVD secret police, was a human cul de sac. For most, there was no way out. Chiszek spent the best part of four years in solitary confinement, under constant interrogation. He writes:

my patience and my self-confidence, even my innate stubbornness, were gradually wearing away. I was tired of the struggle, I was tired of fighting, but above all I was tired of second-guessing myself in the silence of solitary confinement. I was tired of doubts, fears, and the constant anxiety and strain.

He felt abandoned by God. In the end the NKVD 'broke' Chiszek: to get some respite he falsely admitted that, yes, he was a Vatican spy! This was the point of an extraordinary conversion. He was humiliated, guilt-ridden and ashamed by his own weakness. Despite the appalling hunger, the cold and solitary confinement, he had been falsely confident that his will was strong enough to resist anything. In utter desolation he faced the God he had failed:

> I pleaded my helplessness to face the future without him. I told him that my own abilities were now bankrupt and he was my only hope ... I knew that I must abandon myself entirely to his will and live from now on in this spirit of self-abandonment to God. And I did it.

Chiszek was sentenced to fourteen years hard labour in Siberia. Surrounded by the most callous underworld criminals, weak and exhausted by incessant work, always bitterly cold, nothing prevented Chiszek from exercising his priestly ministry in the Siberian Gulag. Knowing that to be caught probably meant

MARTIN TIERNEY

death did not deter him from celebrating Mass furtively in forests or secret bolt-holes. He attracted others who recognised their spiritual desolation and their need of God. To them, his ministry was a miracle of God's providence. Clandestinely, he even managed to conduct retreats, on a one-to-one basis. He writes of this time of suffering:

> I had to have constant recourse to prayer, to the eyes of faith, to a humility that could make me aware of how little my own efforts meant and how dependent I was upon God's grace even for prayer and faith itself.

I don't think all this is irrelevant to today's world. As we are surrounded by a culture alien to the Gospel, and so lacking in the consolation of success, the armour we need is prayer, faith and humility before God. Most of us are certainly not suffering physical deprivation but the temptation to capitulate to the culture we live in is real, both for priests and lay people. To prevent ourselves being 'evangelised' by worldly ways and values, Chiszek's way of seeking always God's will is the only guarantee that we will not fail.

After serving his time, Chiszek, was given limited freedom in a town called Norilsk. He was constantly under surveillance. Closet Christians began to come to him. He wrote:

> I was amazed and consoled by the constancy of these people's faith and their courage in the face of persecution, so I was determined to help them

as long as I could. Even if it meant being arrested again, or being sent back to the camps, I was willing to run that risk in order to serve as a priest for these courageous Christians. I often marvelled at the way these people had clung to the faith in this professedly atheistic country.

Chiszek finally got his freedom through a 'spy swap' between the Russian and American governments.

Survey Reveals Enormous Challenges to Church

A recent survey revealed that many people expressed a need for some sort of faith. Most rejected the traditional faith of their Baptism.

What makes people tick? What are the issues, experiences, worries, fears, beliefs and joys of contemporary Ireland? What is the relevance of spirituality, religion and ultimately Jesus Christ in people's lives? Last year a highly reputable international research company was commissioned to conduct a survey to find out the answers to these questions. The methodology used was to establish seven focus or discussion groups countrywide and, in addition, to conduct a very wide-ranging telephone survey with over 1,000 adults contacted in their own homes. Respondents were selected equitably on the basis of age, sex and social class. On reading the results of this survey I am confident that the pulse of the Irish people was taken and an accurate reading was received.

It is patently obvious from the results that there is a broad backlash against 'institutionalised' religion, particularly Catholicism. That's the bad news and it cannot be sanitised. The good news is that people expressed a need for some sort of 'faith' – a reason for being here – but having a 'named' faith was not important to the majority of the people questioned. Over 32 per cent of those questioned claimed to have their own set of rules. A significant 18 per cent just didn't feel any need for belief in the supernatural.

A typical response to questions about faith went something like this: 'I don't know. I'm Catholic but I wouldn't abide by Catholic rules. I disagree with so much stuff they say … But you have to have a bit of faith in something at the end of the day, even if you don't believe everything they think, because if something does happen what is the first thing you do? Say a prayer.'

The findings present an enormous challenge to the Roman Catholic Church. Personally, I find it hard to grasp just how irrelevant the Church has become to so many people. I go to meetings of church personnel and, quite honestly, the real issues are seldom faced. I have to pinch myself at times and ask, 'Am I living in Disneyland?' We are still engrossed in silly titles like Your Eminence, Your Grace, Your Lordship, Monsignor, Canon and Uncle Tom Cobley – utter irrelevancies to the world in which the Gospel is to be preached. We are busy sacramentalising people for whom the very fundamentals of faith remain obscure. On the infrequent occasions when reality is unavoidably faced the less starry-eyed are chided for pessimism or lack of faith, or for not seeing the bright side of things.

The majority of the people questioned believed that Jesus Christ was God. A significant 66 per cent claimed to have an active relationship with him. For the rest, Jesus, rightly or wrongly, was obscured by the religious teachings that they

MARTIN TIERNEY

claimed were 'drilled into them' and which they now reject. A comment on the findings poses an interesting dilemma for Church leaders: 'Despite the traditional religious "imprint" that seems to exist, and which could present a barrier to new messages coming in, we also saw a substantial segment of society that had rejected the beliefs they were brought up with and were almost yearning for some new way of making faith part of their lives.' A substantial 19 per cent of those questioned could be categorised as 'searching'.

Those who felt they 'didn't feel the need for a spiritual life, and who lived in the here and now' were mostly in the 15–24 age group, students and single males. These are the parents of tomorrow. It is hard to predict when the Lord will raise up a leadership capable of responding to the challenges presented in Ireland today. However, if we, like the apostles, 'cannot but speak about what we have seen and heard' we will find ways of bringing the good news of Jesus Christ to everyone.

THE TYRANNY OF CHOICE

We are faced with the tyranny of choice. It is how we choose that is important.

Ever sat down to breakfast in an American diner? If you have you have probably suffered from choice overload! With your coffee, you can have whole milk, organic, skimmed milk, half 'n' half; eggs well done, over-medium, over-easy, scrambled, poached, sunny-side up – the choice is yours. With your pancakes or waffles do you want hash browns, grits, syrup – maple or walnut, cherry or blueberry topping? I am amazed at the ability of the waitresses to remember the available choices. When you go to the supermarket a vast canyon of cereals stretches to the horizon, a universe of flakes, crunchies, puffs and additives, an overflowing cornucopia of baffling breakfast options. Switch on the television and a bewildering number of channel options leaves you dithering with indecision. To look for a simple pair of jeans you can choose from relaxed fit, easy fit, slim fit, traditional cut, stone washed, drainpipe, turn-ups etc. Nothing is simple when one is confronted with the tyranny of choice. We are beginning to look on choice as a right and we complain

MARTIN TIERNEY

bitterly if our particular brand of bread, cereal, butter or margarine isn't available on the shelf of our local supermarket. In the developed world choice is consumer wallpaper. It's there, we expect it, but it is seldom noticed.

I recall on one occasion returning from Ethiopia with a stopover in Paris. This was at the height of the 1985 famine in that country. On Boulevard Hausmann I visited the chic cathedral of opulence, Gallerie Layfette. I was outraged by the opulence, the garish in-your-face display of everything the world had to offer to pamper 'home sapiens'. In just hours I was whisked through the sky from a place of no choice to the confusion of virtually unlimited choice. I was stunned by the global injustice of our planet. For millions, life hangs by a tenuous thread. At the same time millions more gorge on a surfeit of everything that is supposed to make people happy. Why can we not share our good fortune with others?

There appears to be a growing consensus that our own country is gripped by a greed not seen since the canyon cave man first took residence in Ireland after the Ice Age. Thanks to RTÉ and a *Prime Time* programme on planning, the human face of greed was given flesh. What we saw and heard wasn't pretty. That the poorer sections of our society haven't risen in rebellion is a complete mystery to me. Could it be that things don't change because the poor don't vote?

Last week a newspaper published the Rich List, Ireland's top one hundred wealthiest people. Half of those in the top ten in the list were tax exiles. They aren't even contributing to the common pot that goes to help your aged mother find respite care or your father who is suffering from emphysema find a bed instead of a trolley in the local hospital. Our parish school in urgent need of essential repairs received the princely grant of €11,000! At present, the rampant disease among the rich is status anxiety. It's not enough to have a CL Class Mercedes Coupe in the garage; the latest rage is the Bell Helicopter! All that we have is 'gift'. We are only stewards over our possessions, not owners in a real sense. Thankfully some of the rich have been more than generous in sharing while others remain ever tight-fisted.

I am continually edified by the patient stance towards life adopted by those who have little. In the parish we have wonderful people. Many of them live on widow's pensions or old-age pensions. I can write with absolute honesty that I have never heard them complain. In an age of affluence, their lives are in the main lived in frugality. The unfairness of it all annoys me. Political parties exploit the passivity of those who no longer have the energy or the resources to protest or rebel. If you're not a builder or a developer, if you don't own horses, it is hard to avoid becoming disillusioned with politics. Those with little choice, in my experience, are often the most patient of people. They don't mind lowering their expectation to meet their needs. We live in a country of contrasts.

THE VOICE OF CONSCIENCE

The voice of conscience dies if it is persistently ignored.

Driftwood is as far away from the Kennedys of Castleross as the grainy black-and-white one-channel television was from the current choice of twenty or more satellite stations, all in colour and recordable. *Driftwood* was a ten-minute radio 'soap' from RTÉ. It uncomfortably recorded the foibles of twenty-first century Irish society. It was pacy, even raunchy and pretty accurate. One episode grabbed my attention. Siobhan and Denis Staunton, a married couple expecting a child, lived in Herons Bay where Siobhan was developing a chic and extravagant B&B. When I tuned in they were in the midst of a blazing quarrel. Siobhan had just found out that Denis, who was on a business trip to Manchester, was having an affair. 'So,' Siobhan wailed, 'here I am making sandwiches for you to go off and see your mistress.' Denis replied painfully, 'Siobhan, it was nothing! It was only a conference fling.' Again he pleaded, 'It was nothing!' As the argument boiled it emerged that the mistress was already expecting his child. What struck me forcibly was the phrase, 'it was nothing'. Why did Denis think that being unfaithful to his wife, to whom he had made a life-long commitment, 'was nothing'?

From the tone and force of his voice it was obvious he believed what he was saying. Denis is not untypical. There are many who think the same way. I concluded that Denis, who was not necessarily a bad or evil person, had a dead or dormant conscience.

Conscience is the secret core and sanctuary of every person. It is there one is alone with God whose voice echoes in its depths. Conscience is an integral part of every person. 'Deep within his conscience man discovers a law which he has not laid upon himself but which he must obey. Its voice, ever calling him to love and to do what is good and to avoid evil.' Most people are trained, usually in the home, to obey the voice of conscience. Aided by an instinctive inner voice we know what is right and what is wrong. At the beginning, the voice of conscience is loud and clear. When we deliberately defy the voice of conscience we feel guilty. We then know we are called to repentance and to a change of heart. However, if avoiding, neglecting or defying the voice of conscience becomes a habit of life, the voice grows muffled and dies. Then the heart becomes hardened. In *Driftwood*, I believe Denis was telling the truth, as he saw it, when he claimed that his adultery 'was nothing'. His conscience was no longer functioning. How is it that so many people trot in and out of Tribunals and tell obvious lies on oath? Are they all bad people? Could it be that by neglecting the voice of conscience they have lost the ability to distinguish between right and wrong, evil and goodness? Why do so few people go to Confession? Could it be that they no longer recognise sin for what it is?

Guilt alerts us to a healthy functioning of conscience. If at times you feel guilty, it could mean that you are spiritually the healthiest person alive! It is popular nowadays for trendy

MARTIN TIERNEY

commentators to talk about 'Catholic guilt'. I believe this is an attempt, every so subtly, to denigrate the function of conscience, thereby leaving all moral behaviour neutral. Guilt may call for repentance, healing and a change of life.

If the conscience is dead something needs to replace it, even if only for mental health. Otherwise one's own well-being, fulfilment and pleasure become the only plumb line against which behaviour is measured: if it is good for me it is good; if it is bad for me it is bad. This type of morality leads to a narcissism and selfishness, which, at their core, are empty and superficial. Conscience is a judgement of reason by which we can recognise the moral quality of a concrete act. If we have done bad things and experienced the verdict of our conscience, that is a good thing. It is a pledge of conversion and a sign of hope.

We can form our conscience, especially through our reading of scripture and the teaching of the Church. 'The Word of God is a light for our path.' We need to reflect on the voice of God speaking to us through his word. This is one way in which a moral conscience is formed. I find it a great puzzle that so many passages of scripture are neglected, ignored or defied, even by church-goers. They go blithely on their way as if it were not for them! It is obvious that their unformed consciences are not alert to sense the moral danger of constantly ignoring God's word.

The teaching of the Church also forms our conscience. Jesus said, 'go, therefore teach all nations'. To ignore the teaching of the Church lightly must necessarily carry implications for our position within the Body of Christ and our eternal salvation. We have to be honest with God, with ourselves and with our consciences, if we are to have the peace that Jesus promised.